ACOUSTIC GUITAR MAGAZINE'S PRIVATE LESSONS

ACOUSTIC GUITAR SLIDE BASICS

BY DAVID HAMBURGER

Publisher: David A. Lusterman
Editor: Jeffrey Pepper Rodgers
Managing Editor: Stacey Lynn
Music Editor: Andrew DuBrock
Designer: Trpti Todd
Production Assistant: Christopher Maas
Production Director: Ellen Richman
Marketing: Jen Fujimoto
Music Engraving: Andrew DuBrock
Recording Engineer: Carl Thiel

Cover photograph: Todd Wolfson
Photographs: page 9, courtesy National Reso-Phonic Guitars; pages 10, 11, 15, 23, 38, 47, 55, and 71, Todd Wolfson; page 13, Frank Driggs Collection; page 20, Jay Blakesberg; page 27, Raeburn Flerlage, Frank Driggs Collection; page 42, Joe Alper, Frank Driggs Collection; page 50, Frank Driggs Collection; page 57, Frank Driggs Collection; page 64, Frank Driggs Collection

Contents © 2001 David Hamburger
ISBN 978-1-4234-4578-4

501 Canal Blvd., Suite J, Richmond, CA 94804; (510) 215-0010; Stringletter.com

This is an Errata for page 4. Website provided is incorrect, please following the instructions below to for correct web address to access and obtain audio files for your book.

Go to the Acoustic Guitar website visit http://store.acousticguitar.com/

Then under the search put in Acoustic Guitar Slide Basics-

Results page will say….

Acoustic Guitar Slide Basics: Complete Audio Tracks

This is the complete set of audio tracks accompaniment file for the musical examples and songs in the **Acoustic Guitar Slide Basics** book, and is available as a free download to customers who have already purchased the book. To access files, click on it and there will be a spot to add it to your cart. Once added to your cart it will show as $0.00.

CONTENTS

AUDIO TRACKS

The complete set of audio tracks for the musical examples and songs in *Acoustic Guitar Slide Basics* is available for free download at Store.AcousticGuitar.com/AGSB

INTRODUCTION

Using a slide may be one of the most evocative and expressive ways to coax sound from an acoustic guitar. The roots of the blues are entwined with the roots of slide guitar, and the slide sound has traveled up through most of the largest branches of American music. While there are countless shades of blues—both country and urban, prewar and postwar, solo and band—slide guitar is often considered the epitome of the blues spirit. And the slide pantheon itself is a diverse one, home to both the classic Delta repertoire of Robert Johnson and the bottleneck gospel recordings of Blind Willie Johnson, to both the witty, polished solo instrumentals of the prolific Tampa Red and the evocative landscapes of Ry Cooder's present-day sound tracks.

This book is designed as an introduction to acoustic slide guitar, so even if you have never put bottleneck to strings, you can start here. If you've done a little finger-picking, already play some blues, or have fooled around with open tunings at all, that will certainly help. The focus here is on the fundamentals of playing solo acoustic slide: understanding open-G and open-D tuning; playing fingerstyle (coordinating a melody or chord pattern played by your fingers with a bass pattern played by your thumb); learning various left-hand and right-hand techniques for getting a clean, clear sound with the slide; and using shuffle, straight-eighth, and alternating-bass patterns to play a variety of eight-bar and 12-bar I–IV–V chord progressions. If you don't know what some of these terms mean, hang in there, because by the end of the book you will.

Each chapter of *Acoustic Guitar Slide Basics* introduces you to a particular aspect of playing slide. Short examples throughout each chapter walk you through a progression of licks, phrases, and patterns while highlighting specific musical concepts central to the slide style. Each chapter also includes two or three longer examples in which you put everything together to play a tune.

Slide guitar is one of the great sounds of American roots music and one of the most mysterious to the uninitiated. When you've finished this book, you'll be well equipped to start figuring out recordings or transcriptions and to begin making up some pieces of your own. With a good grasp of the basics, you'll be on your way.

David Hamburger

MUSIC NOTATION KEY

The music in this book is written in standard notation and tablature. Here's how to read it.

STANDARD NOTATION

Standard notation is written on a five-line staff. Notes are written in alphabetical order from A to G.

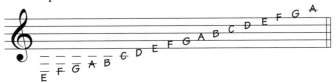

The duration of a note is determined by three things: the note head, stem, and flag. A whole note (○) equals four beats. A half note (♩) is half of that: two beats. A quarter note (♩) equals one beat, an eighth note (♪) equals half of one beat, and a 16th note (♪) is a quarter beat (there are four 16th notes per beat).

The fraction (4/4, 3/4, 6/8, etc.) or c character shown at the beginning of a piece of music denotes the time signature. The top number tells you how many beats are in each measure, and the bottom number indicates the rhythmic value of each beat (4 equals a quarter note, 8 equals an eighth note, 16 equals a 16th note, and 2 equals a half note). The most common time signature is 4/4, which signifies four quarter notes per measure and is sometimes designated with the symbol c (for common time). The symbol ¢ stands for cut time (2/2). Most songs are either in 4/4 or 3/4.

TABLATURE

In tablature, the six horizontal lines represent the six strings of the guitar, with the first string on the top and sixth on the bottom. The numbers refer to fret numbers on a given string. The notation and tablature in this book are designed to be used in tandem—refer to the notation to get the rhythmic information and note durations, and refer to the tablature to get the exact locations of the notes on the guitar fingerboard.

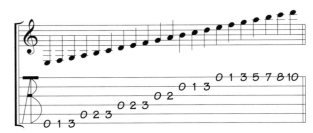

FINGERINGS

Fingerings are indicated with small numbers and letters in the notation. Fretting-hand fingering is indicated with 1 for the index finger, 2 the middle, 3 the ring, 4 the pinky, and T the thumb. Picking-hand fingering is indicated by i for the index finger, m the middle, a the ring, c the pinky, and p the thumb. Circled numbers indicate the string the note is played on. Remember that the fingerings indicated are only suggestions; if you find a different way that works better for you, use it.

CHORD DIAGRAMS

Chord diagrams show where the fingers go on the fingerboard. Frets are shown horizontally. The thick top line represents the nut. A Roman numeral to the right of a diagram indicates a chord played higher up the neck (in this case the top horizontal line is thin). Strings are shown as vertical lines. The line on the far left represents the sixth (lowest) string, and the line on the far right represents the first (highest) string. Dots show where the fingers go, and thick horizontal lines indicate barres. Numbers above the diagram are left-hand finger numbers, as used in standard notation. Again, the fingerings are only suggestions. An *X* indicates a string that should be muted or not played; 0 indicates an open string.

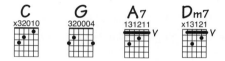

CAPOS

If a capo is used, a Roman numeral indicates the fret where the capo should be placed. The standard notation and tablature is written as if the capo were the nut of the guitar. For instance, a tune capoed anywhere up the neck and played using key-of-G chord shapes and fingerings will be written in the key of G. Likewise, open strings held down by the capo are written as open strings.

TUNINGS

Alternate guitar tunings are given from the lowest (sixth) string to the highest (first) string. For instance, D A D G B E indicates standard tuning with the bottom string dropped to D. Standard notation for songs in alternate tunings always reflects the actual pitches of the notes. Arrows underneath tuning notes indicate strings that are altered from standard tuning and whether they are tuned up or down.

VOCAL TUNES

Vocal tunes are sometimes written with a fully tabbed-out introduction and a vocal melody with chord diagrams for the rest of the piece. The tab intro is usually your indication of which strum or fingerpicking pattern to use in the rest of the piece. The melody with lyrics underneath is the melody sung by the vocalist. Occasionally, smaller notes are written with the melody to indicate the harmony part sung by another vocalist. These are not to be confused with cue notes, which are small notes that indicate melodies that vary when a section is repeated. Listen to a recording of the piece to get a feel for the guitar accompaniment and to hear the singing if you aren't skilled at reading vocal melodies.

ARTICULATIONS

There are a number of ways you can articulate a note on the guitar. Notes connected with slurs (not to be confused with ties) in the tablature or standard notation are articulated with either a hammer-on, pull-off, or slide. Lower notes slurred to higher notes are played as hammer-ons; higher notes slurred to lower notes are played as pull-offs. While it's usually obvious that slurred notes are played as hammer-ons or pull-offs, an *H* or *P* is included above the tablature as an extra reminder.

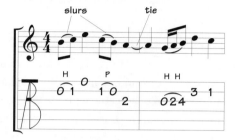

Slides are represented with a dash, and an *S* is included above the tab. A dash preceding a note represents a slide into the note from an indefinite point in the direction of the slide; a dash following a note indicates a slide off of the note to an indefinite point in the direction of the slide. For two slurred notes connected with a slide, you should pick the first note and then slide into the second.

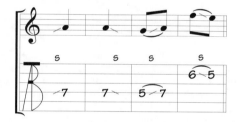

Bends are represented with upward curves, as shown in the next example. Most bends have a specific destination pitch—the number above the bend symbol shows how much the bend raises the string's pitch: ¼ for a slight bend, ½ for a half step, 1 for a whole step.

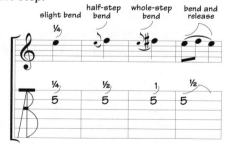

Grace notes are represented by small notes with a dash through the stem in standard notation and with small numbers in the tab. A grace note is a very quick ornament leading into a note, most commonly executed as a hammer-on, pull-off, or slide. In the following example, pluck the note at the fifth fret on the beat, then quickly hammer onto the seventh fret. The second example is executed as a quick pull-off from the second fret to the open string. In the third example, both notes at the fifth fret are played simultaneously (even though it appears that the fifth fret, fourth string, is to be played by itself), then the seventh fret, fourth string, is quickly hammered.

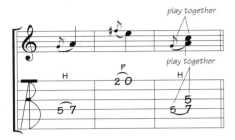

HARMONICS

Harmonics are represented by diamond-shaped notes in the standard notation and a small dot next to the tablature numbers. Natural harmonics are indicated with the text "Harmonics" or "Harm." above the tablature. Harmonics articulated with the right hand (often called artificial harmonics) include the text "R.H. Harmonics" or "R.H. Harm." above the tab. Right-hand harmonics are executed by lightly touching the harmonic node (usually 12 frets above the open string or fretted note) with the right-hand index finger and plucking the string with the thumb or ring finger or pick. For extended phrases played with right-hand harmonics, the fretted notes are shown in the tab along with instructions to touch the harmonics 12 frets above the notes.

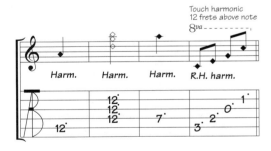

REPEATS

One of the most confusing parts of a musical score can be the navigation symbols, such as repeats, *D.S. al Coda, D.C. al Fine, To Coda,* etc.

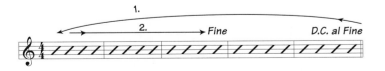

Repeat symbols are placed at the beginning and end of the passage to be repeated.

You should ignore repeat symbols with the dots on the right side the first time you encounter them; when you come to a repeat symbol with dots on the left side, jump back to the previous repeat symbol facing the opposite direction (if there is no previous symbol, go to the beginning of the piece). The next time you come to the repeat symbol, ignore it and keep going unless it includes instructions such as "Repeat three times."

A section will often have a different ending after each repeat. The example below includes a first and a second ending. Play until you hit the repeat symbol, jump back to the previous repeat symbol and play until you reach the bracketed first ending, skip the measures under the bracket and jump immediately to the second ending, and then continue.

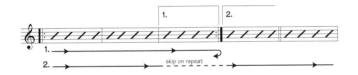

D.S. stands for *dal segno* or "from the sign." When you encounter this indication, jump immediately to the sign (𝄋). *D.S.* is usually accompanied by *al Fine* or *al Coda. Fine* indicates the end of a piece. *A coda* is a final passage near the end of a piece and is indicated with ⊕. *D.S. al Coda* simply tells you to jump back to the sign and continue on until you are instructed to jump to the coda, indicated with *To Coda* ⊕ .

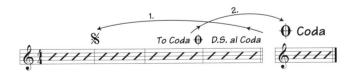

D.C. stands for *da capo* or "from the beginning." Jump to the top of the piece when you encounter this indication.

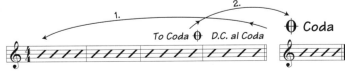

D.C. al Fine tells you to jump to the beginning of a tune and continue until you encounter the *Fine* indicating the end of the piece (ignore the *Fine* the first time through).

GUITARS, SLIDES, AND TUNINGS

Before we actually start playing slide, you need to get geared up and ready. Let's look at what kind of guitar you need, what the optimum setup is, how to pick out a slide, and how to get into the open tunings we'll be using in this book.

SIZE AND SCALE LENGTH

Sorry, but playing slide doesn't necessarily mean that you have to buy a new (or old) guitar. You can literally play slide on any kind of guitar, but some guitars will work much better than others. To narrow it down a little, steel strings are going to work much better than nylon strings. They'll sustain better with a slide, and they'll get more of that characteristically "slide guitar" tone. After that, scale length and setup are the most important factors. Scale length is the distance from the nut to the bridge, and generally, the longer it is, the stiffer the strings feel under your fingers. Different models of guitars have different scale lengths; for example, dreadnought-style guitars have a longer scale length, while jumbo-style and smaller-bodied guitars tend to have shorter scale lengths. Small-bodied guitars are prized by fingerpickers for the easier, springier feel their shorter scale length provides, but that's not necessarily the best thing for playing slide. Why not? Well, let's look at what's going on when you start to use a slide.

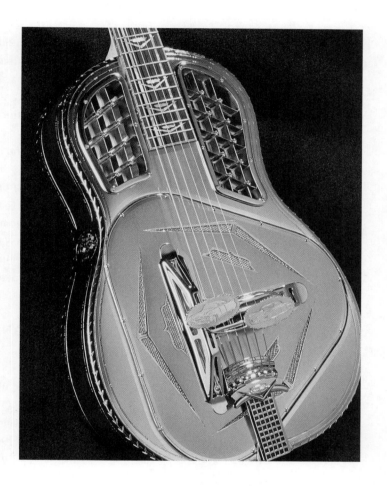

National Reso-Phonic '59 Fins tricone.

SETTING UP FOR SLIDE

When you play slide, you move the slide along the strings without actually pressing the strings to the fretboard. Higher action, light-gauge strings (.012 on top) or heavier, and the stiffer response of a longer scale length guitar all contribute to an easier setup for slide because they create more resistance when you press the slide to the strings. There's more holding you back, so you can dig in with the slide, making stronger contact with the string (which is good) without getting so close to the fretboard that you start knocking into the frets as you slide up or down the strings (which is bad).

"Cool!" you think to yourself. "I'll just use that old guitar of mine with the totally warped neck and the cheese-grater action—you couldn't get those strings within half an inch of the fingerboard without using a C-clamp." Well, you could, and some people do actually prefer cheap guitars for slide—they say these instruments create a more "authentic" tone, more like what the early bluesmen played. But here's the tricky part. You want to clear the frets easily with the slide, but unlike a Dobro or lap steel guitarist, you're still going to be fretting *some* notes with your fingers. So you don't want an instrument that's completely unplayable the conventional way. It is nice to have a spare instrument you can just leave in an open tuning while you learn, so you might want to score some kind of just-playable steel-string for that purpose.

DOBROS AND NATIONALS

In the late 1920s the Dobro and National guitar companies began making metal- and wood-bodied instruments with various sizes and combinations of cones, or resonators, built into the faces of those instruments. These metal cones, shaped like speaker cones, were designed to acoustically amplify the instrument's output, and the resulting sound was distinctly different from a flattop guitar's. Many bluesmen have used resophonic guitars over the years, but during the Depression such instruments were generally beyond the budget of all but the most successful musicians. So while Tampa Red, with his string of hokum hits, could sport a fancy engraved tricone, most musicians cranked it out on more affordable Stellas, Regals, or whatever else was at hand. Robert Johnson posed with a Gibson flattop, and even that may have been borrowed; whatever he did record with, it's generally agreed that it wasn't a resophonic instrument. So while the National sound is a significant part of the picture, it's hardly the whole story. Which ultimately just means that, all those album covers to the contrary, you don't actually need a vintage resophonic guitar to get going. (Nice try.)

CHOOSING AND WEARING A SLIDE

You *will* need to get a slide, and there are many kinds to choose from. You'll need to try out a few different diameters, lengths, and materials to see what suits you best. Most acoustic slide guitarists place the slide on their pinkie, leaving three fingers free for forming chords and fretting single notes without the slide. Placing it on your ring finger lets you grip the slide from both sides, with your middle finger and pinkie, but it leaves you with only two fingers free for chording and fretting without the slide.

Generally, the heavier the slide, the better the tone, with a higher "note-to-buzz" ratio. At the same time, a heavier slide is harder to manipulate—there's more to move around, and if your guitar still has relatively light strings or low action, it's going to take more finesse to keep a heavier slide from bumping into the fretboard. But weight is just part of an equation that also includes what the slide is made out of.

The two classic slide materials are glass and metal. Some of the first slides were made from the tops of wine bottles (hence the term *bottleneck guitar*) or from lengths of pipe (hence the term . . . er . . . *metal slide*). Glass tends to have a smoother, rounder sound; the distinction is particularly noticeable on the lower, wound strings, where a metal slide can get really raspy. A thick and hefty brass slide will have more smoothness to it but can be a lot of weight to haul around the fretboard at first. Thin-walled glass slides will just sound plinky, with almost zero sustain, and thin metal slides, usually steel with a chrome coating, will be equally difficult to coax a great sound from. If you've been using one of these, yes, you can blame your gear.

Ceramic and porcelain slides are a more recent development offering the best of both glass and metal: they're smooth and relatively light like glass, but they feel denser and offer a touch and sustain more reminiscent of metal. They're a little on the fragile side, chipping and cracking easily if you don't take especially good care of them. Meanwhile, there are various small manufacturers making heavy, hand-blown glass slides, slides made from real bottlenecks, and various kinds of tapered and curved brass slides as well, all of which are worth checking out.

As for the size of the slide, it's easiest to continue to fret chords and single notes if the slide covers just the first two joints of your pinkie. This means finding a slide that fits snugly enough that it comes to a stop right above your second knuckle, yet is long enough to cover all six strings when you lay the slide across the fretboard (see photo below). Anything longer will just make it that much harder to sense where your finger is inside the slide, which in turn will affect your sense of where to place the slide to cover a particular string or fret. Anything shorter will make it impossible to play a full chord with the slide across all the strings, or to cover bass notes with the slide while playing a melody on top.

TUNINGS

We're going to work in the two most essential slide tunings, open G and open D. Just to give your ears a few reference points, open G is the tuning for Son House tunes like "Death Letter" and "Empire State Express," early Muddy Waters recordings on Chess including "Mean Red Spider," "Can't Be Satisfied," "Long Distance Call," and "Little Geneva," and, when capoed or tuned up three half steps to B♭, Robert Johnson's "Walkin' Blues" and "Come On in My Kitchen." It's also the tuning Bonnie Raitt uses on "I Feel the Same" and "Shadow of Doubt." Open D is the tuning for Blind Willie Johnson's "Dark Was the Night" and "Nobody's Fault but Mine"; all of Elmore James' work, including "Dust My Broom"; much of Ry Cooder's slide work on *Boomer's Story, Into the Purple Valley,* and *Paradise and Lunch;* and, when raised up a whole step to E, Tampa Red's "Denver Blues" and "Things 'Bout Comin' My Way."

Following are explanations of how to get into open-G and open-D tuning from standard tuning. You may also find yourself wanting to go from one open tuning to another, so there are also step-by-step explanations of how to get from open D to open G and vice versa. When written out, the notes of each tuning are listed from the sixth string up to the first string (i.e., from the lowest, heaviest string to the highest, lightest string). For example, standard tuning would be written out as E A D G B E, low to high.

D and G tuning involve lowering three or four strings, including the sixth string. Instead of starting from the sixth string and working up to the top as we would for standard tuning, we're going to use harmonics to check the strings we have to change against the ones that remain constant. You make a harmonic by touching your finger to a string directly over the fret, without pressing it to the fretboard, and lifting your finger from the string as soon as you've picked the note. Of course, the audio downloads include a set of tuning tracks, so you can work directly with them or use them to check your progress with the methods described on page 12.

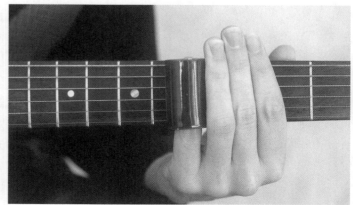

TUNING TO OPEN D FROM STANDARD TUNING

Tuning to Open D

Open D is D A D F♯ A D, low to high.

1. Lower your sixth string a whole step to D.

   Check: 12th-fret harmonic, sixth string = open fourth string

   Or fifth-fret harmonic, sixth string = 12th-fret harmonic, fourth string

2. Lower your first string a whole step to D.

   Check: 12th-fret harmonic, fourth string = open first string

   Or fifth-fret harmonic, fourth string = 12th-fret harmonic, first string

3. Lower your second string a whole step to A.

   Check: 12th-fret harmonic, fifth string = open second string

   Or fifth-fret harmonic, fifth string = 12th-fret harmonic, second string

4. Lower your third string a half step to F♯.

   Check: Fourth fret, fourth string = open third string

Strum across all six strings, bottom to top, and you should hear a nice D chord

TUNING TO OPEN G FROM STANDARD TUNING

Tuning to Open G

Open G is D G D G B D, low to high.

1. Lower your sixth string a whole step to D.

   Check: 12th-fret harmonic, sixth string = open fourth string

   Or fifth-fret harmonic, sixth string = 12th-fret harmonic, fourth string

2. Lower your first string a whole step to D.

   Check: 12th-fret harmonic, fourth string = open first string

   Or fifth-fret harmonic, fourth string = 12th-fret harmonic, first string

3. Lower your fifth string a whole step to G

   Check: 12th-fret harmonic, fifth string = open third string

   Or fifth-fret harmonic, fifth string = 12th-fret harmonic, third string

When you are in tune, you should be able to get a good-sounding G chord by strumming across the strings starting with the fifth string.

TUNING TO OPEN G FROM OPEN D

To D G D G B D from D A D F♯ A D.

1. Tune your fifth string down a whole step, from A to G.

   Check: Seventh fret, fifth string = open fourth string

2. Tune your second string up a whole step, from A to B.

   Check: Third fret, second string = open first string

3. Tune your third string up a half step, from F♯ to G.

   Check: Fifth fret, fourth string = open third string

TUNING TO OPEN D FROM OPEN G

To D A D F♯ A D from D G D G B D.

1. Tune your fifth string up a whole step, from G to A.

   Check: Fifth fret, fifth string = open fourth string

2. Tune your second string down a whole step, from B to A.

   Check: Seventh fret, fourth string = open second string

3. Tune your third string down a half step, to F♯.

   Check: Fourth fret, fourth string = open third string

SINGLE-STRING MELODIES

Guess what? After all the time you've spent learning to finger chords without looking or to play lead lines without thinking too hard, now you've got a piece of metal, glass, or ceramic encasing one of your four valuable fingers. When you place this object on the strings, you can't tell at first how hard you're pressing it or if you're pressing it against the strings at all. Hmm. Makes playing a little confusing, doesn't it? Let's take a look at what's going on when you play guitar this way to get a better sense of how to handle the slide and what to listen for as you do it.

When you play with a slide, you don't want to press the string down to the fretboard. When the slide makes contact with the string, the effect is the same as pressing the string into contact with a fret: the string length is shortened, creating a higher pitch. This means that to get a pitch with the slide that matches the pitch you'd get with a fretted note, you need to be *right over the fret,* not in between two frets as you would be without the slide. It is having the slide, not a fret, stop the string that makes slide guitar sound like slide guitar, because unlike a fret, you can move the slide while the note is still vibrating. That's how you get the unique sound of slide guitar: it's the sound of a string's pitch being moved fluidly, with no step-by-step increments, from one pitch to the next.

Make sense? So you've got to really pay attention to your touch—how heavily or lightly you bear down on the strings with the slide. And there's more: since the pitch you get from the string is the direct result of where you place the slide on it, your *intonation* matters now. That means that not only does your guitar need to be in tune, but *you* need to be in tune—you need to be able to hear if you're at the pitch you want. You can do a certain amount of slide placement by sight, but to play slide convincingly requires learning your way around with your ears as well.

Your fretting hand can help too. While it's true that you've got this *slide* coming between you and strings, and you don't have the feel of the frets to guide you, you've still got your thumb riding along the back of the neck when you play, and your index finger riding along the strings behind the slide (more on that later). You can use these to stay oriented so that you don't feel like your fretting hand is just floating in space.

OK. Having said all that, let's see what it actually feels like to play a little slide.

Gospel bluesman Blind Willie Johnson.

FIRST SLIDE

We're going to begin in open-D tuning: from the sixth string to the first, D A D F♯ A D. If you need a quick refresher on getting into this tuning, see page 12. Otherwise, just tune down and then compare your open strings against track 2 to make sure you are in tune.

Open D is a good beginning point for slide, because it allows you to play a wide range of melodies without ever leaving the high string, and the high string is the easiest string to play cleanly on with the slide. Let's start by placing the slide directly over the fret you want. Play Example 1 on page 14 by placing the slide on the high string directly over the fourth fret each time there's a four in the tablature and playing the open high string in between (the zeros in the tablature).

Angling the slide to play only the high string.

Tuning: D A D F# A D

TRACK 4 Ex. 1

The slide doesn't have to cover all six strings, nor do you have to use the end of the slide closest to your palm if you're just playing the high string. With these single-string exercises, you can get a cleaner sound by angling the slide so that it's touching *only* the high string (see photo). The idea is to cover only the strings you're actually applying the slide to.

Right. So let's get some practice dropping the slide onto the string in more than one place. Example 2 is made up of part of the D-major scale:

TRACK 5 Ex. 2

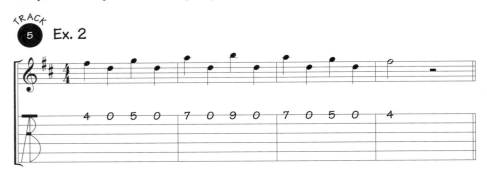

I hear you say, "This is swell, Dave. When are we going to actually *slide* on the strings?" An excellent point. Well, sliding is pretty much a matter of accurately getting *to* a specific place by moving along the string *from* a specific place. Dig, as the jazz cats say, Example 3—a slide from the second to the fourth frets.

TRACK 6 Ex. 3

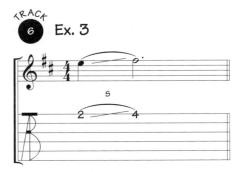

Now, as if it were a tongue twister, do that ten times fast. What happens? Are you getting lots of open high-string noise in between? Maybe some clank or rattle or buzz as you come back into the second fret or as you come off of the fourth fret to start over again?

Try this: The index finger on your slide hand has nothing better to do right now, so let it ride along the strings behind the slide. See if you can get it to land on the strings just before your slide does and get it to leave the strings just after the slide does. The idea is to have your index finger act as a damper on the open strings, keeping them from ringing when the slide is in transition between notes. This is called *left-hand damping* (see photo).

Note: If you're already doing this intuitively, great. Meanwhile, make sure you're not keeping the slide on the string in between landing at the fourth fret and going back to the second. In other words, you don't want to be just sliding back and forth between the second and fourth frets without ever lifting the slide.

Try this over a few more notes, as in Example 4.

The index finger lands on the strings before the slide and keeps them from ringing out.

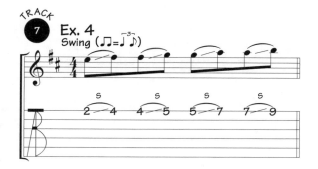

GRACE NOTES, MUTING, AND OTHER ESSENTIALS

Sometimes you're playing two distinct notes, as in Example 3, and sliding from one to the next. Other times you might slide into a note just for the sound of sliding into it. In other words, the first note is something you blow through to get to the second note. In that case, there are first and second notes but the first note is just part of the sound of getting to the second, slid-into note.

Confused? Check out Example 5 on paper and in the audio, and then we'll discuss it.

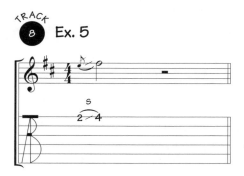

All right. Unlike Example 3, the point here is just the fourth fret, the F♯. The E, at the second fret, is what the classical folks call a *grace note*. It's the note that flavors the F♯, giving you that nice, honkin' slide up from below.

Try grace-noting your way into all the notes we covered in Example 2, as in Example 6. Watch your step on the way back down in particular. Then it's time to add in a little right-hand coordination. In Example 7, while continuing to play grace-note slides, repeat each note that you land on three more times while holding the slide in place.

Remember to use that left-hand index finger as a damper, especially on the jump from the seventh fret back to the fourth fret in measure 2.

Your right hand can take care of muting the strings as well. You can effectively and completely stop a note from ringing out by bringing your picking finger back to rest on the same string after you play it. In Example 8, use your picking finger to mute the string after each pair of eighth notes, creating a beat of rest each time. I know you'll be stunned to learn that this is called *right-hand muting.*

So far we've done our sliding in one direction only, and we've used left-hand damping or right-hand muting to give us time to move the slide back down the string. But there are reasons to slide in the other direction as well. Play Example 9, and notice the attention it takes to accurately pull the slide *back* to the pitch you started from:

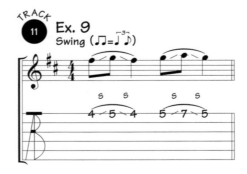

Example 9 is a situation in which you can use your fretting-hand thumb to stay oriented. Plant your thumb at a comfortable point on the back of the neck and play at the fourth fret. Without moving your thumb from its spot, slide up to the fifth fret, stretching your hand. Then bring the slide back to the fourth fret. Move your hand, including your thumb, up to a point where you can do the same kind of stretch from the fifth to the seventh fret and back, and so on (see photos).

Try this in conjunction with a grace-note slide. Example 10a shows a quick slide up to the fifth fret before sliding back to the fourth fret at the beginning of the next measure. Example 10b is the same idea a couple of frets up.

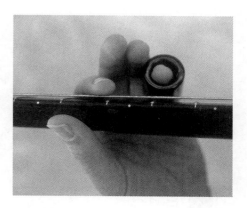

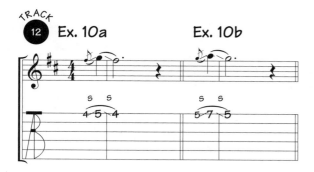

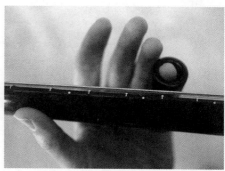

The thumb stays planted while the slide moves up.

The next two examples illustrate how you can start putting some of these different ideas together to make musical phrases. In Example 11a, pay attention to your left-hand damping on the jump from the fifth fret to the grace note starting on the second fret.

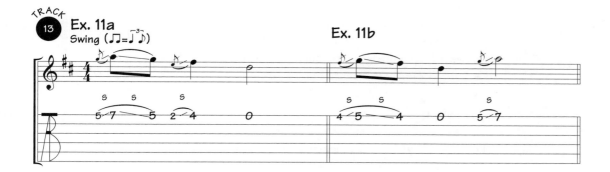

TRIPLETS

While music is made up of all kinds of rhythmic values in all kinds of configurations, it's amazing what you can accomplish with a handful of humble eighth, quarter, and half notes. The key is *phrasing*—how the notes are placed across the beat. Even in Example 10 you can hear the impact of beginning a phrase before the downbeat, or 1, of a measure.

Triplets, as the name implies, tend to surface in threes. You can have triplets of any kind of note—quarter-note triplets, half-note triplets, eighth-note triplets. Imagine three big gangsters in matching checked suits trying to squeeze into a two-seater convertible (imagine bucket seats while you're at it). That's what triplets are like—they are three notes trying to squeeze themselves into the space of two.

Look at and listen to Example 12. In the first half of the measure, we've got two pairs of regular eighth notes. Then, in the second half of the measure, we've got two sets of eighth-note triplets. Any three eighth-note triplets take up the same amount of time as two regular eighth notes, but they squeeze in an extra note, and all three notes are the same length. Very sneaky.

So what good are they? Well, check out the lick we can get in Example 13 by incorporating a triplet rhythm into a series of now-familiar slide moves.

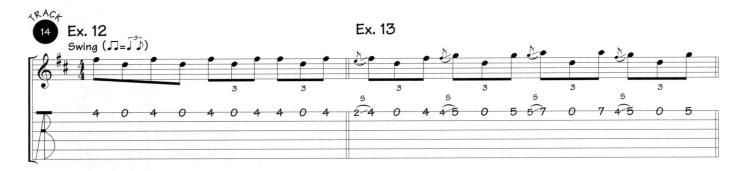

CUCINA BLUES

Before we wrap up with a short song, let's sum up the elements we've introduced in this chapter:

- Place the slide directly over the fret.
- Use the left-hand index finger for damping the strings.
- Angle the slide when playing only on the high string, so that you touch only the high string with the slide.
- Distinguish between sliding between two full-valued notes and using a first note as a grace note into a second, main note.
- Use your picking finger to mute a string.
- Use your fretting-hand thumb as a pivot when sliding to and from a note in the same phrase.

These are many of the key elements of slide playing. Congrats—you're on your way.

Now try your hand at an eight-bar blues melody entitled "Cucina Blues." This tune may remind you of an eight-bar blues by Robert Johnson, the one whose lyrics involve lost love, a suggestion, and the threat of inclement weather.

CUCINA BLUES

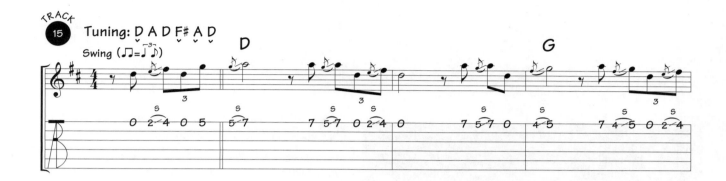

WORKING IN THE THUMB

Versatile slide man Ry Cooder.

One of the main reasons to play slide with your fingers is so you can provide backup for yourself: once you've got some funky melodies going with the slide, you can get the bass going with your thumb at the same time. After you work through this chapter, you'll be able to thump out a steady quarter-note groove on the low string while continuing to syncopate cool licks on top. The first step is finding the bass notes with the thumb; next comes using the thumb to keep a steady bass groove going. Once you can do that, it's a matter of learning to play licks with the slide without losing track of the bass part your thumb is playing. If you take it in steps, it can be done, and more important, being able to do so will make you *tres* popular at parties.

Let's start with the opening lick of "Cucina Blues" from the last chapter. This time, we'll play it as a *call and response*. How does that work? In Example 1, your fingers play the melody with the slide, just like before (that's the *call*), and this time you answer with two bass notes, played by your thumb (that's the *response*).

To better hear where those bass notes are falling in each measure, repeat Example 1 a number of times, as in Example 2, until you can keep it going with a good sense of groove:

Raising the stakes just a little more now, try dropping in these bass-note responses while playing a sequence of two *different* melody phrases, or the first two measures of "Cucina Blues," as in Example 3.

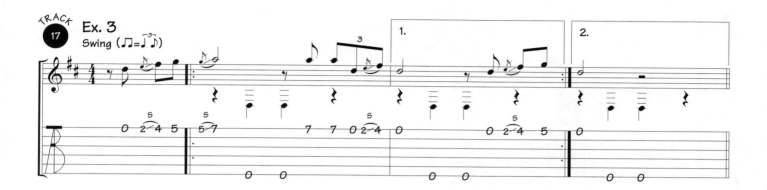

At this point, you may have guessed what's next. Yep, you could play the entire eight-bar blues at the end of the last chapter using this call-and-response approach. Here it is, laid out for your reading and playing pleasure, in Example 4:

STEADY ON

"Great," I hear you say, "but what if I want to keep the bass going all the time? Can it be done?" At this point, I could respond in one of two ways. I could look around, lower my voice, hunch over the table, and hand you a dirty, chipped glass slide made out of the last whiskey bottle Charley Patton drank from. Then I could press a torn and faded map of the Mississippi Delta into your hands and tell you that you may never see me again, and the camera would cut to reveal a posse of bad guys and hellhounds waiting for me in the driving rain at the crossroads on the way out of town.

Or, I could just say, "Yep. Read on."

I hate unnecessary drama, so I'm going with the second answer. The best way to get a steady bass going is to take it step by step. Start by hitting quarter notes with your thumb on the low string. Bonk, bonk, bonk, bonk. Just as in Example 5. Then add the high string on the first beat of each measure, using your index or middle finger, as in Example 6. We call this right-hand technique a *pinch*: you are picking simultaneously with your thumb and finger, and the two digits are moving toward each other, as in, you guessed it, a pinch.

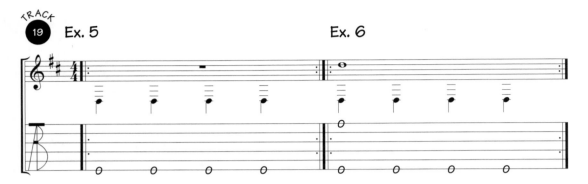

Once you've got that coordinated and can do several groovy, in-time repetitions in a row, make that note on the high string a slide note, as in Example 7. Then do half notes: keep the thumb thonking away and play a slide note on beats 1 and 3, as in Example 8. Next proceed to quarter notes, as in Example 9: slide into the first note, and then keep picking with the slide at the fourth fret for the next three notes. Notice that you're now pinching with your thumb and finger on every beat.

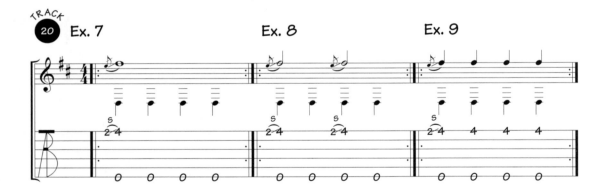

Let's make things even more interesting. In Example 10, you are still keeping the thumb going like clockwork and playing quarter notes on the high string, but now it's a different note on the high string each time. So you're moving the slide around and picking with your finger while maintaining the low end at the same time. Really, you should have considered the circus if you can do all this.

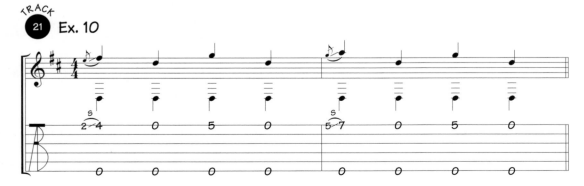

Let's pull all this into a tune—call it "Steady Now." This is another eight-bar blues; this time the melody reaches up to the 12th fret and the notes come out of the D-minor pentatonic scale. If you care to think about such matters, observe the ♭7 of the scale (C♮) at the tenth fret and the ♭3 (F♮) at the third fret—these are those "blue notes" you read about in the *Harvard Dictionary of Music*.

STEADY NOW

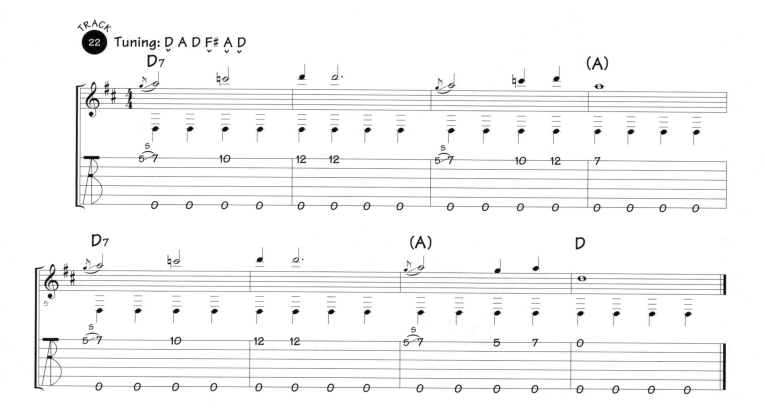

RIGHT-HAND DAMPING

And now for more discussion of right-hand technique. *Right-hand damping* (not to be confused with the already-discussed right-hand muting) accomplishes two things: it gives you a more solid attack by anchoring your right hand on the face of the guitar, and it creates a thumpier and faster-decaying sound on the low strings.

To damp the bass strings with your hand, let the fleshy part of your palm—the part that moves with your thumb—rest on the bottom few strings right where those strings meet the bridge of the guitar. Experiment by sliding your hand more onto the bridge or more toward the soundhole and then picking the bass strings with your thumb to hear the different degrees of muting you can get. Compare this with the way the strings sound when you hold your hand completely off the face of the guitar. The ideal sound, if we can say one exists, is one in which the strings are neither completely cut off nor completely ringing out but are somewhere in between. You want to hear the notes, and have them ring long enough to hear their actual pitch, but to decay quickly.

Right-hand damping helps keep the bass notes from drowning out the melody, and it increases the impression that you're playing two different things at once by sharpening the difference in timbre between the bass notes and the high strings. Listen to Example 11, in which you can hear first undamped and then damped bass notes.

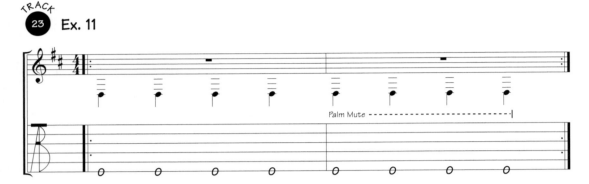

Go back to some of the earlier examples in this chapter and listen to the difference when you consciously apply right-hand damping to the bass notes.

EIGHTH-NOTE MELODIES

For our next trick, we're going to get our fingers moving faster than our thumb. Example 12 involves playing eighth notes in the melody over a steady quarter-note bass. Note that you only have to slide twice per measure, on the downbeats of 1 and 3:

The important thing to listen for right now is if you're flip-flopping: playing the eighth notes on the low string with your thumb instead of on top with your fingers. "Not me!" you exclaim. And maybe not. But it can be tricky to read the tab, play the notes, and listen to yourself analytically at the same time, so it is always a good idea to tape yourself occasionally and listen back to what you're doing. For any kind of fingerstyle playing, it's essential to have control at all times over what you're playing in the bass and to be able to maintain that regardless of what you play on top.

Most often in a real musical situation you'll find yourself mixing it up in the melody between eighth notes and quarter notes; one way to sharpen your reflexes is to practice going back and forth between the two—as in Example 13.

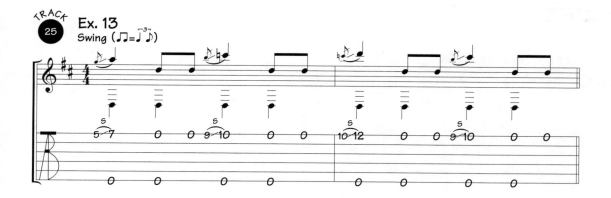

PLAYING ON THE OFFBEAT

Melodies often call for beginning a phrase on an *offbeat*—on the *and*, as the jazz cats like to say: "1 *and* 2 *and* 3 *and* 4 *and*." Example 14 provides you with some practice playing all offbeats over steady bass notes that stay *on* the beat. Example 15 is one more exercise along these lines, in which we combine eighth notes on the downbeat with eighth notes on the offbeat.

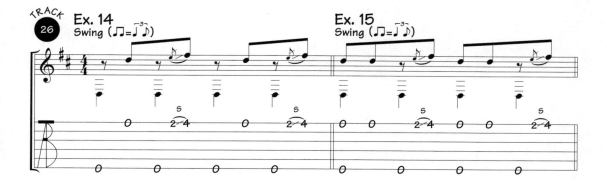

"Offbeat Blues," on page 26, is another blues with a D-minor pentatonic melody. It includes some slippery eighth-note action, with most of the melody notes in measures 4–6 falling on the offbeats. Compare this with "Steady Now" to see how much of a difference it makes just having control over where the eighth notes are placed. For more practice playing offbeat eighth notes over a steady bass, try taking just measure 4, measure 5, or measure 6 and playing it in a loop.

OFFBEAT BLUES

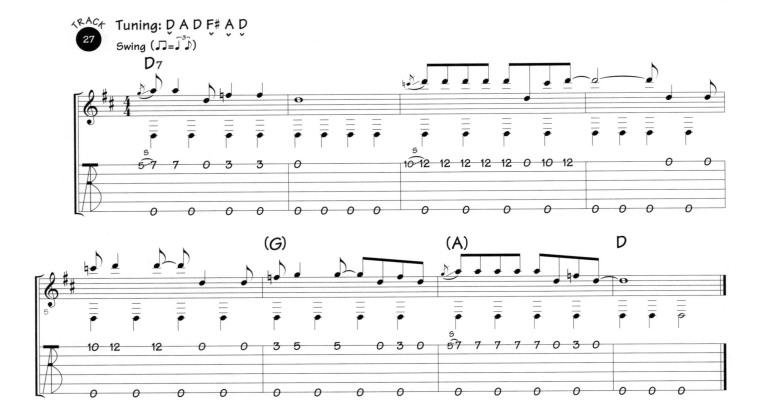

OPEN-G TUNING AND CLOSED POSITION

For this chapter and the next one, we're going to switch from open-D tuning to the other most common tuning for acoustic slide, namely open G. Low to high, the notes are D G D G B D. See page 12 for tips on retuning your guitar to open G, and check your pitches against track 3.

Bluesman Bukka White, 1970.

So far we've been using the slide on one string, creating melodies up and down the high string and always coming back to the open high string. We're going to begin in open G using the slide *across* the top three strings, playing everything up at the 12th fret (where the notes are conveniently the same as the open strings, but an octave higher). This is called playing in *closed position,* because there are no open strings involved—every note is played with the slide.

Because we'll be using more than one string to play melodies, it will be helpful to assign one picking finger to each string: try using your index finger for the third string, your middle finger for the second string, and your ring finger for the high string. This is only a starting point; try this approach as you work through the examples in this chapter, but if something else seems more comfortable to you, try that out as well. Example 1 is a good exercise for getting used to this picking system.

Tuning: D G D G B D

STRING TO STRING

Working on more than one string makes it possible to slide into one string and then pick an adjacent string. "Why," I hear you ask, "would I want to do that?"

Well, because it's *cool,* as you can hear in Examples 2 and 3. Example 4 is a slightly more elaborate move, with an additional same-string slide at the end.

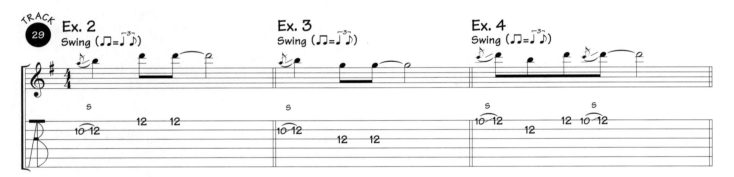

In Example 5 you slide up on the B string to land on the high string, then slide up on the B string again to land on the third string; in Example 6 you land first on the third string, then on the high string:

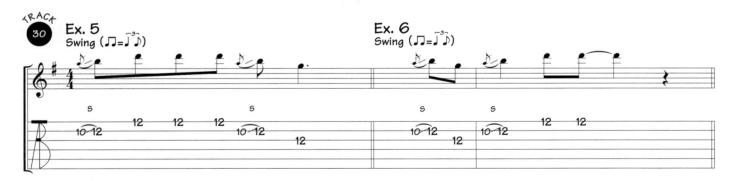

TRANSPOSING

Transposing means changing the key of something while keeping it rhythmically and melodically intact. In other words, you're moving every note in a phrase, a lick, or a whole piece up or down the same amount. (When you put a capo on a guitar at the second fret, you're transposing everything up a whole step: your G chord becomes an A chord, and so on.) All the licks we've played so far in open G involve two or three of the top three strings, and therefore, because of the tuning, they spell out most or all of a G-major chord. They'll sound great over a G chord or a G note in the bass, but what if we want to go to another chord? No problem; playing slide in an open tuning makes it easy to transpose those licks to another position.

"A likely story," you say. "Last time someone told me things were going to be easy, I found myself swaying in the breeze 50 feet above the ground on the ropes course at summer camp, hanging on for dear life." OK, you've got a point. But there's nothing here to give you vertigo, except maybe the lofty music theory involved, and you can always ignore that and just play the notes. So let's see a little transposing in action.

Playing the top three strings at the 12th fret spells out a G chord, or the I chord in the key of G. If we want to imply or spell out a D chord, or the V chord in the key of G, all we need to do is move the slide down five frets, to the seventh fret position, and play the same licks. The three basic notes in Example 7a we'll now play as the three notes in 7b:

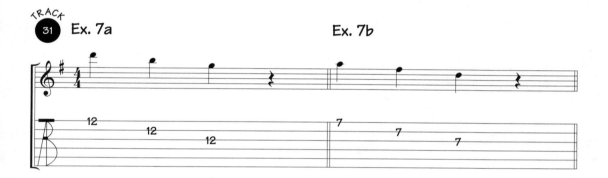

Therefore, a lick like Example 8a will become the lick in 8b:

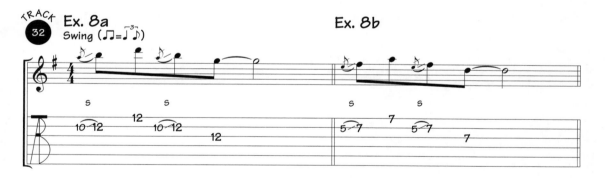

Which means we can now play the whole 16-bar groove in "From Twelve to Seven." This up-tempo shuffle rocks back and forth between the I chord (G, with licks at the 12th fret) and the V chord (D, with licks at the seventh fret). Note that when you're playing in D and based around the seventh fret, you're going to go *below* the seventh fret, down to the fifth fret, to slide into the notes you want. Think about it like this:

Chord	Played at	Slide from
G	12th fret	10th fret
D	7th fret	5th fret

FROM TWELVE TO SEVEN

RETURN OF THE TRIPLETS

We've already tangled with triplets in D tuning; now we're going to hear how they sound in closed position, in G tuning. I hear you say, "Well, how *do* they sound?" And the answer is: "Pretty cool." They just take a little fancy fingerwork to come off properly. Take Example 9 out for a spin.

TRACK 34 **Ex. 9**

Things move pretty quickly when you're playing triplets. The main issue in Example 9 is getting back down to the 10th fret on the B string each time you're about to make the upward slide again. If you mute the high string with your ring finger after the last note in each triplet, you can move the slide quickly back to the tenth fret without hearing any extra sounds from the high string.

Example 10 mixes triplets with quarter notes. In this example, the tricky part is sliding up to the 12th fret at the end of each triplet and then sliding from the tenth to the 12th fret on the high string for the grace note into the quarter note. If you tilt the slide to play on the high string while damping with your left-hand index finger, you won't hear any extra sounds from the second or third string.

TRACK 35 **Ex. 10**

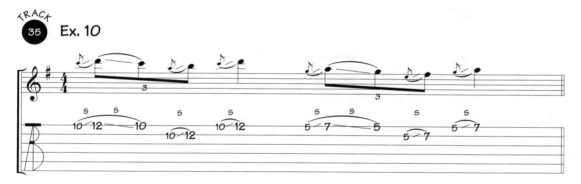

VIBRATO

Vibrato is that subtle (or not-so-subtle) quavering of pitch that happens on sustained notes, especially at the end of a phrase. It's tempting to say that you can figure out vibrato only by hanging out on street corners, in poorly lit pool halls, or down by the docks in the bad part of town near the abandoned freight yard with the one-armed conductor who's seen only on Halloween. But there is an identifiable technique to it, although probably everybody has a different way of describing it. Here's mine.

Vibrato sounds like an effortless undulation of the slide, but you can actually develop that effortless sound by practicing a series of very specific, controlled slides. These are slides made down from the note you're applying the vibrato to and back up to it. There are times when you want a wide, almost out-of-control buzz around the note you're playing, but to get that subtle, vocal-like vibrato that caresses the note without sounding out of tune, it's key to consider the point directly over the fret as the absolute top of your motion with the slide. All motion away from that point goes only below and back up to that point. Try Example 11. After you pick the note at the 12th fret, dip the slide a bit below the 12th fret.

Next, pick at the 12th fret, dip the slide below the note, bring it back up, and dip it again before picking again, as in Example 12. Then make those dips happen twice as rapidly and pick the string half as frequently, as in Example 13. The motion of the slide itself against the string should help to sustain the note at this point.

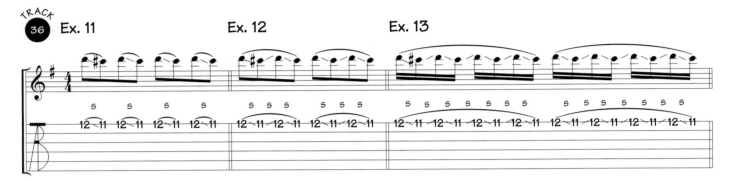

While you should be able to count and feel the 16th notes go by, the next step is to go beyond countable notes to create a subtle hum of motion as you move the slide back and forth. When that is happening (and be patient—you might work on this for days or weeks before it suddenly jumps into your hands), try Example 14. The idea is to slide into a note, hold it a moment, and then bring it to life with a little vibrato:

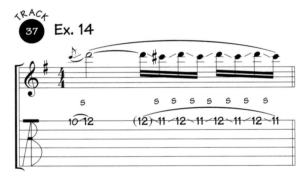

Note: For the sake of these exercises, I have notated the vibrato motion as a 16th-note slide from the 12th fret to the 11th and back again; normally it is indicated with a squiggly line above the staff. The distance and speed of the vibrato are up to you.

THE IV CHORD

So far we've dealt with just the I and the V chord. But transposing makes getting to the IV chord just as easy as getting to the V chord. In the key of G, the IV chord is C, and in open-G tuning we can find the notes we need to spell out a C chord at the fifth fret, as shown in Example 15:

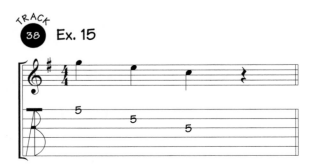

We're moving triad notes around the same way we did when we started going to the V chord. So a lick in G like Example 16a becomes a lick in C (Example 16b) when played at the fifth fret:

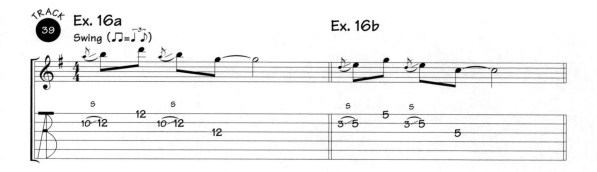

For licks in C, or the IV chord, all your slides will start two frets below the fifth fret—that is, you'll begin at the third fret and slide up to the fifth fret.

In our closing tune, "Transposin' and Tumblin'," the V-chord (D) figure at the seventh fret in measure 2 is transposed down a whole step to become a IV-chord (C) figure in measure 4. There isn't a whole lot of time to work in any vibrato until the two long G notes at the end, at the beginning of measure 7 and measure 8. There are, however, plenty of triplets and several of the string-crossing slides we've been working on.

TRANSPOSIN' AND TUMBLIN'

SPICING UP YOUR MELODIES

Delta master Robert Johnson.

We've been playing melody notes with the slide as far down as the third string in open G. To add in a bass-string root note we need to use the G at the open fifth string. The combination of bass notes on the fifth string and melody notes as low as the third string means that you will often have as little as only one unused string between bass and melody notes. Your mission now is to learn how to handle the slide so that you can get those melody notes on the second or third string without the slide interfering with the bass notes.

We'll start by just getting familiar with placing closed-position notes over a steady bass on the fifth string. Play each measure of Example 1 several times to get the feel of sliding into each string over the G bass note.

Tuning: D G D G B D

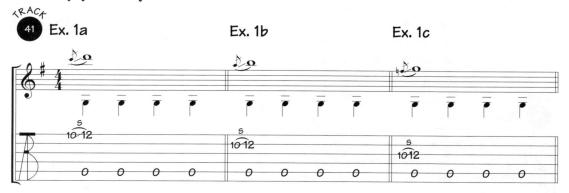

If you have trouble hitting the fifth string clearly and consistently, work on just playing bass notes with your thumb before starting to add in the slide notes on top with your fingers.

In Example 2, you're changing strings on top every two beats. Work on getting to where you can play this one smoothly several times in a row. Then proceed to Example 3, in which you're playing twice as many notes—one quarter note on top for every quarter note in the bass—but only sliding into every other note. Example 4 is about placing eighth notes in the melody over a quarter-note bass, while sliding only into the first and fifth notes of the measure. Try this rhythmic pattern on the second and third strings, too.

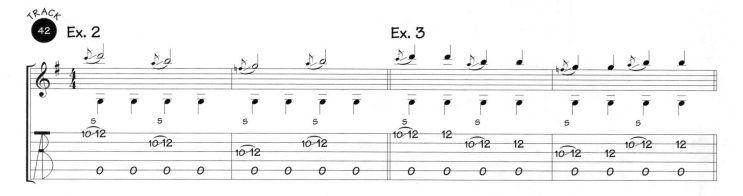

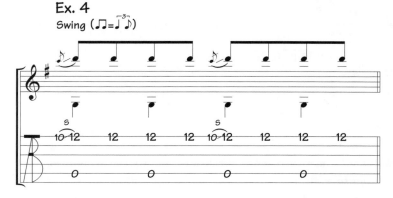

In Example 5, you're placing triplets over the bass notes. As with Example 4, you can also practice this pattern on the second and third strings. Examples 6a and 6b take a couple of those string-crossing moves from the last chapter and synchronize them with a steady bass. Example 7 gives you a little more practice with this idea, while incorporating triplets as well.

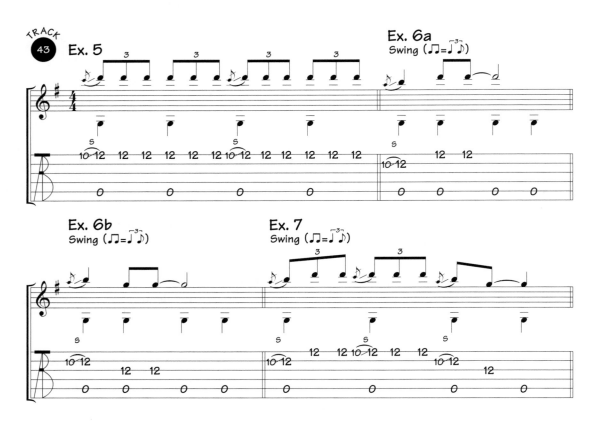

Here's a longer example, the kind of thing you might play for the first four bars of a 12-bar progression:

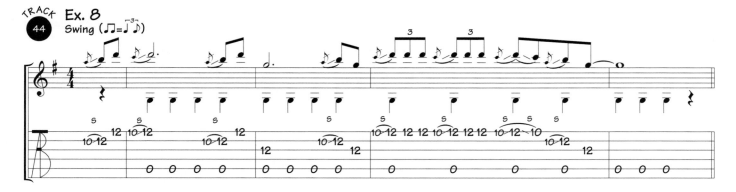

In the last chapter, we transposed I-chord licks into V-chord licks by moving them down five frets, to the seventh fret. This turned our G licks into D licks. To keep a steady bass going under those D licks, or V-chord licks, just drop your thumb down to the lowest string, which, in open-G tuning, is a D. We've got D licks, and we've got a D bass note. How cool is that? So we can turn Example 9 into Example 10.

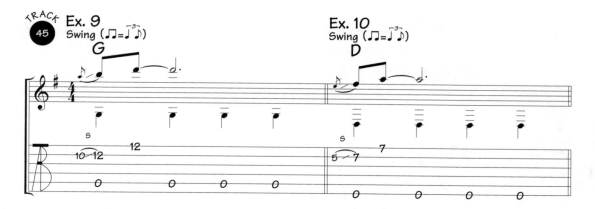

Practice switching your thumb back and forth between the fifth and sixth strings (Example 11a), then add the slide on top (Example 11b).

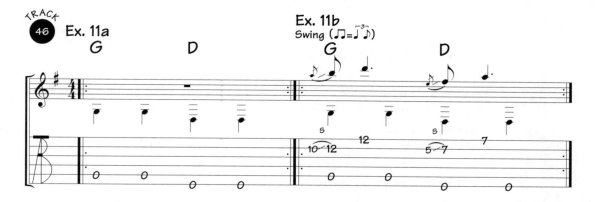

RHYTHMIC ANTICIPATIONS

As often as not, melodies don't start squarely on the downbeat but sometime before or after. At the beginning of a tune, if the melody starts before the first beat, that means you're starting to play with your fingers before the bass notes (and your thumb) have come in at all. In the middle of a tune, a *rhythmic anticipation* like this means you may be beginning a I-chord lick with the slide at the 12th fret while your thumb is still picking out D's on the sixth string (for the V chord) or beginning a V-chord lick at the seventh fret while still picking G's on the fifth string (for the I chord).

See Example 12. You come in at the beginning with the first melody note right before the first bass note of measure 1. At the end of measure 1, you've got to get down to the seventh fret while you're still playing G in the bass, and at the end of measure 2 it's backto the 12th fret while you're still finishing up the last D bass note.

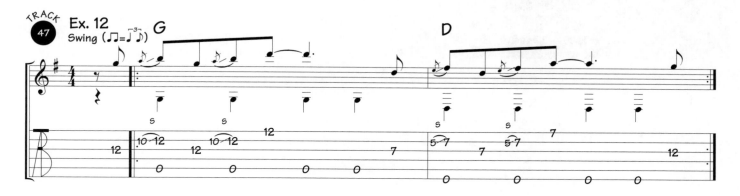

Example 13 uses the same idea, only the pickup begins even sooner, so you're changing position with the slide three eighth notes before the bass changes. The best way to get a grip on this is to take one of these two-measure licks and play it as a loop.

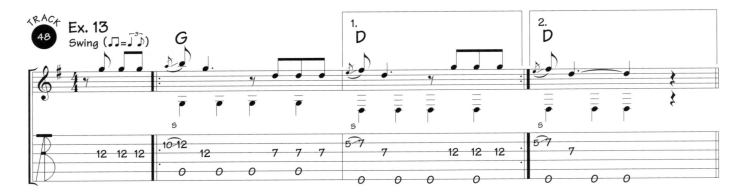

RIGHT-HAND DAMPING AND SLIDE PLACEMENT

Remember right-hand damping? The idea was to get the palm of your picking hand anchored in just the right place where the strings meet the bridge to get that thumpy bass-note sound that isn't totally muffled. This is tricky enough in open D, where you're only thinking about the lowest string. In open G, you've got to balance the placement of your hand so that you're not entirely muffling the sixth string *or* letting the fifth string ring out too much. The only secret here is there is no real secret; it's mostly a matter of trial and error. Experiment with the placement of your hand, listening to what each bass string sounds like as you pick with your thumb.

Keeping the slide out of the way of the bass strings.

Meanwhile, you may have noticed that when you're playing on more than just the high string, you have to pay close attention to keeping your slide out of the way of the open fifth and sixth strings. You can't angle the slide as you would to play on just the high string, but you can still get a clean sound on the top three strings by playing with the end of the slide toward the tip of your finger, so that none of the slide is extending past the third string (see photo). This is also pretty much trial and error; you're looking for a positioning of the slide that allows you to get the notes you need and no more, and to get those notes to ring true while not scraping against any of the bass strings below.

Think on these things as you turn to the eight-bar blues called "Three-Note Jump," which starts out on the V chord. Try using palm muting for all the bass notes. The melody anticipates the chord in the next measure with a three-eighth-note phrase in measures 2, 4, and 6 and in the pickup to measure 1.

THREE-NOTE JUMP

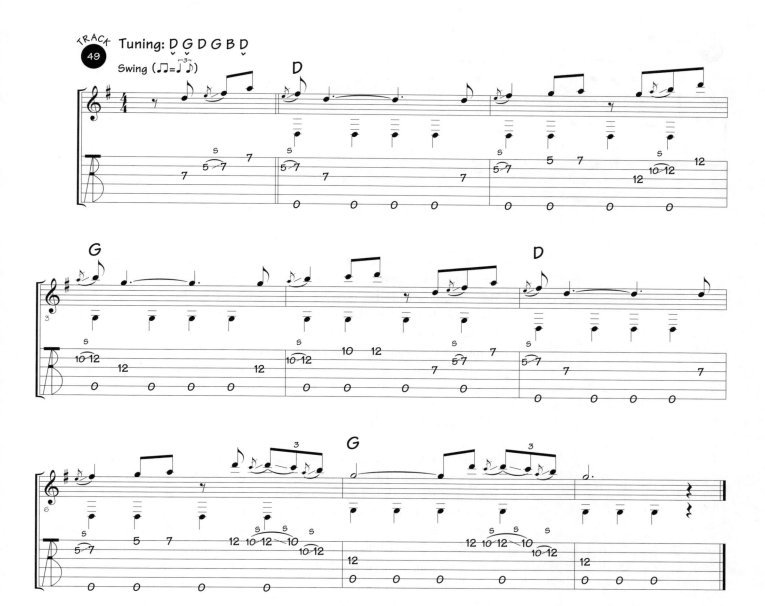

FINESSING THE V CHORD

If you're slick, you don't actually have to change positions for the V chord. "What?" I hear you say. "You tell me this *now*, after all that hard work?!" Relax—it's still important to know how to change positions for the V. All I'm saying is that there are ways to use the 12th-fret position to play ideas that will work well over the V chord.

The best way to understand this is just to hear and play an example. Why, look—I happen to have one right here, Example 14. Note the quick turnaround from I to V and back again in measures 3 and 4, calling for some rapid thumb work:

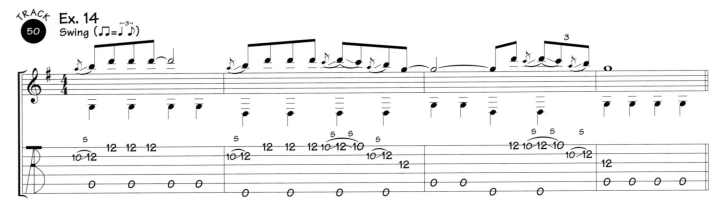

Why does this work? Well, when you stick to the notes at the 12th fret like this, you're basically playing notes from a G-major scale. That still sounds all right over the V chord because the V chord and the I chord are both in the *key* of G, and both chords are built out of notes from the G-major scale. Also, when you're passing fairly quickly through the V chord like this, the sheer melodic strength of repeating a figure in the G-major scale over both chords will carry you through.

Besides, just listen to it. It *sounds* good. Sometimes that's enough of a reason.

SEVENTH-CHORD LICKS

We should take a look at one other move, and that's the incorporation of two notes *above* the seventh fret position while playing over the V chord. Witness Example 15. Playing at the tenth fret on the second and first strings will give us the 5 and ♭7, respectively, of a D chord. (If this makes no sense to you, sit tight for a moment.) This position makes possible certain tangy, "seventh-sounding" licks as in Example 16.

Why does that position sound so good? Well, the top note you're playing, the tenth fret on the high string, is the ♭7 of a D chord. Think about when you're playing a regular open-position D-major chord in standard tuning, and then you switch to an open D7 chord. That one note you're changing to, C, is the note we're adding in here, too. And that sound, the seventh-chord sound, is a stronger V chord sound than just a

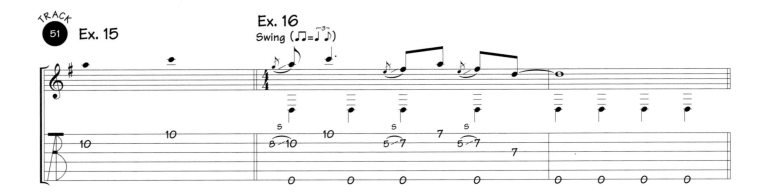

regular major V chord. The D7 sound wants to take you somewhere—specifically, it wants to return to the I chord, or G. So when you play a lick like Example 16, it will sound more satisfying when you then return to the 12th fret and a G in the bass.

You can hear the same tug from D7 toward G in our little tune called "Two-Chord Draw." As you dig in, observe the three-note anticipation of the downbeat before measure 1 and in measure 4. Note also the way that you slide from the ninth fret into the tenth fret to use our new V-chord position. This example, like Example 14, also starts on the V chord.

TWO-CHORD DRAW

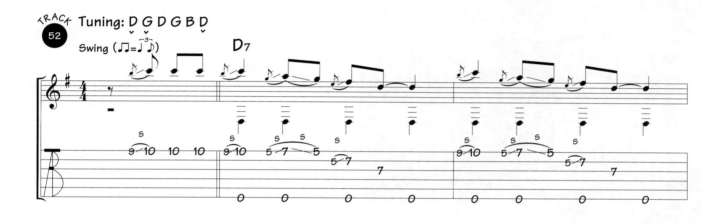

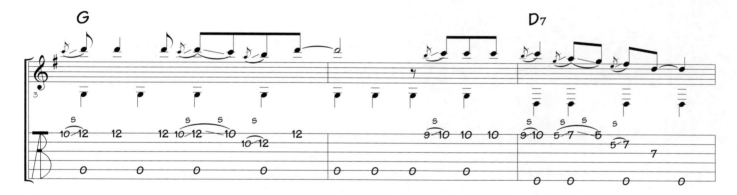

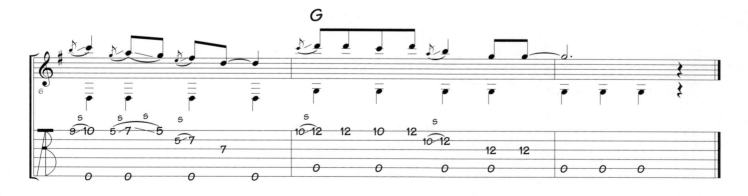

SHUFFLING IN D

Eddie "Son" House at the Newport Folk Festival, 1965.

We have been zipping around the neck in open-G tuning, playing in closed position, and now it is time to do the same in open D. Remember open-D tuning? While you're retuning to open D, let me explain what's going to happen in this chapter. First, you're going to grumble about having to retune again, after working your way through two chapters in open G. To which I will reply that I have my own brilliant if inscrutable reasons for organizing this book the way that I have. Next, as you proceed to the kitchen for snacks instead of retuning, you will miss the rest of this paragraph's explanation, which goes like this: First we're going to learn a new rhythm for your thumb, the shuffle rhythm, and play some closed-position licks over that. Then we'll work on combining open- and closed-position licks and generally expand our open-position vocabulary along the way.

Alright. You're back? Got your snacks? Let's go, and try not to get crumbs in your soundhole.

WHAT'S A SHUFFLE, ANYWAY?

The shuffle is the essential blues rhythmic pattern, that one that goes "*dow,* da *dow,* da *dow,* da *dow,* da," or maybe "*dump,* da *dump,* da *dump,* da *dump,* da." Say one of those out loud when there's no one around to overhear you and you'll know what I'm talking about.

How do we do that on the guitar? The shuffle pattern all happens with the right-hand thumb. You're doubling up the rhythm on the bass string, playing eighth notes instead of quarter notes. Example 1 shows what a measure of shuffle bass sounds like. (Note: the exercises in this chapter are all meant to be played with consistent right-hand damping.)

It's a good idea to get used to playing different-length melody notes with your fingers across the steady bass shuffle pattern your thumb is laying down, just like we did earlier with the quarter-note bass. Play each measure in Example 2 until you can play it several times in a row without stumbling.

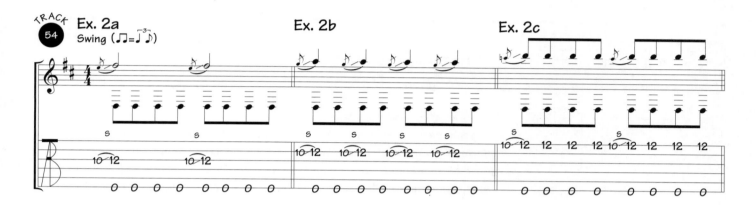

One thing we didn't explore in our first look at open D was playing across the strings at the 12th fret, like we did in open G in subsequent chapters. We're going to do so now; Example 3 gives the four notes we're going to begin working with.

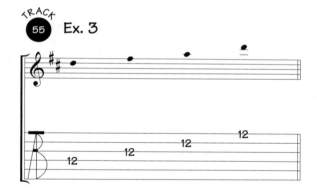

If you think about these notes in terms of what *interval* of the tuning they represent— the root, the third, or the fifth—you'll see that playing closed-position licks in open D is in some ways just a matter of shifting everything you know in open G down one string (see diagram below).

Play the two licks in Example 4; they should sound familiar (if you didn't sneak past the opening exercises in "Open-G Tuning and Closed Position"). In open D, everything is down one string from where it would be in open G. So you have to reach with your right-hand index finger down to the fourth string, which may feel awkward at first. You also have to get the slide to cover the fourth string, without laying it so far over that it interferes with the bottom string.

But the biggest difference between playing in closed position in G and playing in closed position in D is that in D tuning, when you lay the slide across the top four strings and play a chord, you've got a root on top. When you play a chord in open-G tuning, the top note in the chord is only the fifth. Having a high root on top means you can play things like Example 5.

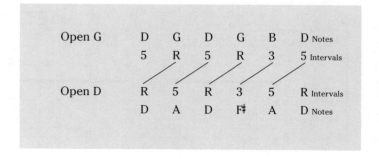

Open G	D	G	D	G	B	D Notes
	5	R	5	R	3	5 Intervals
Open D	R	5	R	3	5	R Intervals
	D	A	D	F♯	A	D Notes

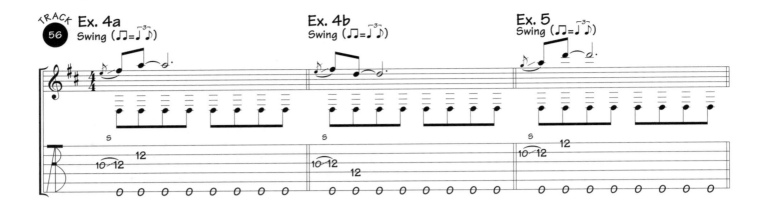

"Yeah, yeah," I hear you say. "I found that lick while I was noodling around this afternoon on the back porch. What else have you got?" Well . . . try out Examples 6 and 7. Neither is any more complicated than the licks we played in the last chapter, but the addition of the root on the high string makes a whole new family of sounds possible.

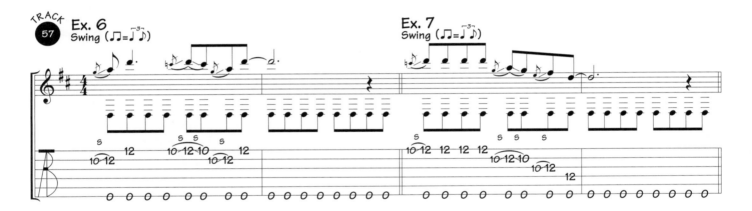

PRACTICE TIP

When working on a new lick, try isolating the movement of your right hand from the notes of the lick. For instance, rhythmically, Example 7 looks like Example 8a. By temporarily removing the selection of strings and slide moves from the picture, you can focus on how the syncopations in your fingers feel against the steady shuffle of your thumb. Then you can walk through the lick placing your fingers on the right strings but still just using open strings, not worrying about the slide, as in Example 8b.

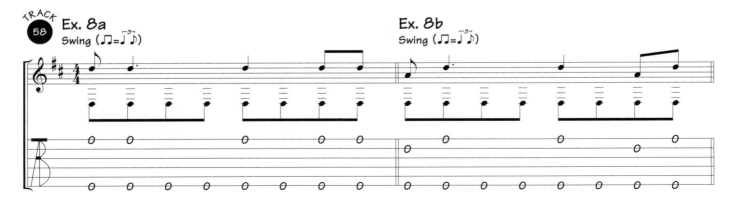

Now when you add in the slide with all the right fret positions and moves, you're not struggling to comprehend three different things at once.

SLIDING INTO THE IV AND V

Now we're going to add in some licks on the IV and the V chords while keeping the bass going with the thumb. To pull off that trick, we need a bass note, a G, to play when we go to the IV chord. And we don't have one on any of the open strings in open D, either. So here's the solution: we're going to play a low G with the slide.

"Get back, Loretta!" I hear you say. "Can it be *done?*" Indeed it can, and here's how. If you place the slide across all six strings, you can cover the bass note you want on the sixth string with the slide, keep it going with your picking thumb, and play licks on top with your fingers. Check out Example 9a to see for yourself. What's more, you can shift the whole thing up two frets and use the same idea to play over the V chord, covering an A with your slide on the low string, as in Example 9b.

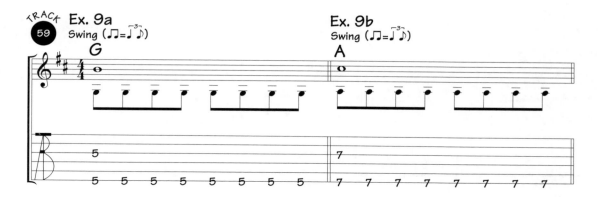

Now the thing is, when you go for a slide lick in closed position while using the slide to cover the bass note as well, you'll wind up sliding into the bass note too. This is completely acceptable and totally cool. So playing a slide lick like Example 10 is going to sound like Example 11 when you add in the shuffle bass.

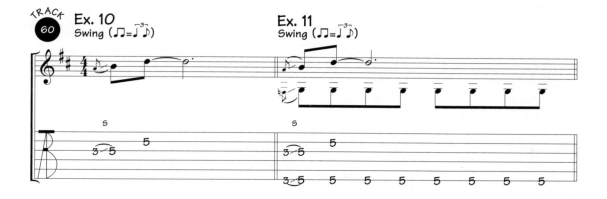

You're still using the open D (sixth) string for the bass whenever you're on the I chord, so the thing to remember is that you'll be moving the slide over onto the sixth string when you go up to a IV or V chord, and pulling it back enough to leave the low string open when you return to a I chord. Use Example 12 to practice these switches.

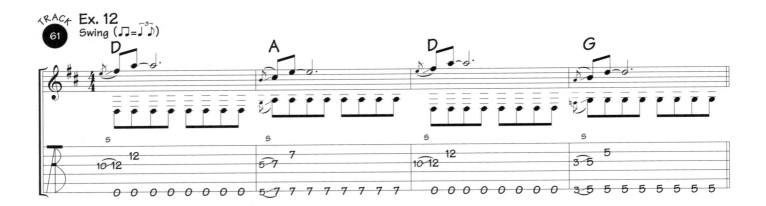

Now try "The Cover-up," paying attention to when you have to cover the sixth string with the slide and when you don't. In this eight-bar blues, all the licks are in closed position. Notice the slides into the bass notes in measures 3, 4, and 6:

THE COVER-UP

MORE IN OPEN POSITION

When we worked in open D in the first couple of chapters, we basically played up and down the high string only. That was a form of open-position playing, in that we just played single notes that generally resolved to the open D string. Now let's add in a few more notes on the second and third strings down near the nut. This is also considered open-position playing because everything is based around the sound of the third, second, and first strings when they're played open, and we're rarely spelling out a chord across the strings with the slide the way we would at the 12th fret. This is, I admit, a pretty slippery definition of *open position,* but this is roots music, after all. You can play first and discuss it afterward.

To begin, we'll add in three notes on the second string (Example 13). Note that the fifth fret on the second string is the same D note as on the open high string. In addition to playing that open D on the high string, we can slide into that same note from below by playing it on the second string, as in Example 14.

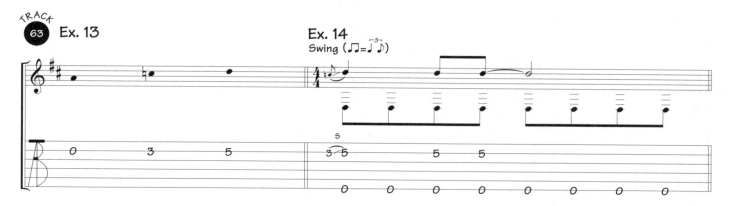

You may find that you're picking up the sound of the high string when you slide up on the second string. Left-hand damping can help: let your left-hand index finger hit the strings just before the slide lands on the third fret to begin its slide up, and you won't get as much of the high string coming along for the ride. Right-hand muting will help too: you can rest your right-hand middle or ring finger on the high string while you pick the second string to prevent the high string from making any sound.

PICKUPS REVISITED

Remember pickups, those rhythmic anticipations we worked with a few chapters ago? Example 15 starts with a pickup, and when you repeat it at the end of measure 1, you've got to coordinate it with your shuffle thumb. To practice this, try taking it ridiculously slowly, just matching up each note of the pickup with a bass note. If you look at it this way, in slow motion, the end of measure 1 works out like three basic pinches in a row: bass note and open second string, bass note and slide at the third fret, bass note and open high string.

Following this kind of open-position lick with a full six-string slide into a closed-position IV or V chord would probably make you one of the more chic people on your block. You owe it to yourself to at least take a swing at it. Example 16 awaits you:

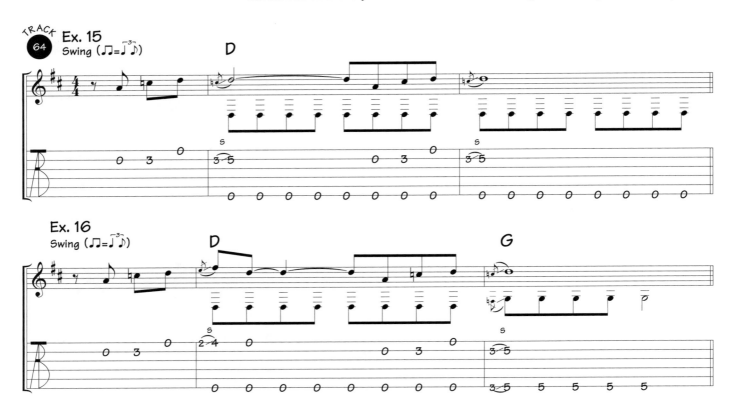

AND NOW, A TURNAROUND

It seems shocking that we've gotten this far without doing any turnarounds yet—those happening little passages that bring you from the end of a chordal cycle back to the beginning—but there you are. Just another example of the rapid decay of ethics and style in these modern times. Well, here is a little tune I will call "Better Late Than Never," in honor of the turnaround in the closing two measures. Again, if you look at measures 7 and 8 as a series of right-hand pinches, it will not seem so mysterious. The descending bass line on the fifth string is fretted in the ordinary way, without the slide; you *will* use the slide for the V-chord lick over the last three beats of measure 8. Other highlights: we begin with open-position licks incorporating the second string and include a seventh-sounding lick at the third fret in measure 2 before moving up into closed position for the IV and V chords.

BETTER LATE THAN NEVER

TRAVIS PICKING

Thumbpicking bluesman Tampa Red.

Travis picking, named for the guitarist, singer, and songwriter Merle Travis, is also called *pattern picking* or the *alternating-thumb* (or *alternating-bass*) style. As that last name suggests, Travis picking involves alternating with your thumb between two strings, and thus two bass notes, while you're on any given chord. So it's a pretty big change from thumping out a shuffle groove on a lone bass string.

The most important thing about Travis picking is keeping the alternation consistent. As you alternate your thumb between two bass strings, you want to play the lower string on beats 1 and 3 and the upper string on beats 2 and 4. Check out Example 1, which shows how to alternate with your thumb between the sixth and the fourth string on a D chord.

Like the shuffle, Travis picking also sounds good with palm muting; you'll have to experiment with your picking hand to get the right balance of muffle and ring on both the sixth and fourth strings.

Once you can play Example 1, it's time to start coordinating your fingers with your thumb. In Example 2, you're going to pinch the high string each time you play the low string; in between, you follow up with the upper bass note on the fourth string. In Example 3, every beat is a pinch: sixth string and first string, fourth string and first string, sixth string and first string, fourth string and first string.

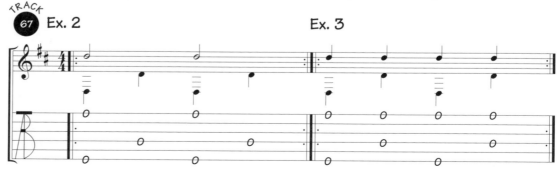

Dave's Practice Advice for these examples is similar to what I said about learning the shuffle pattern: play each of these examples in a loop until you can maintain a hypnotic groove with each one. (When you can succesfully hypnotize the nearest roommate, family member, or casual acquaintance into bringing you a bowl of kettle-style salt-and-vinegar chips and the frosty, age-appropriate beverage of your choice, move on.)

The eighth-note rhythm in Example 4 crops up frequently in the Travis style. To break it down, think of it as a pinch followed by a finger note and then a bass note played alone (no fingers involved). Then you repeat the whole thing.

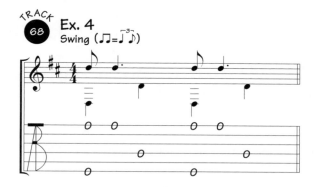

Now, since I hear a little grumbling in the back, let me just say, "No, I haven't forgotten that playing *slide* is still the reason we've all gathered here today." I was, um, getting to that. Let's work in the slide over this alternating-thumb pattern. Example 5 is rhythmically the same as Example 2, only the first of the two notes is played with a by-now-familiar slide move.

Remember the difference between a grace-note slide and a slide between two full-valued notes? In Example 6, the slide in measure 1 is a quick grace-note slide just like the one in Example 5, while the slide in measure 2 is from a full eighth note at the second fret up to the dotted quarter note at the fourth fret.

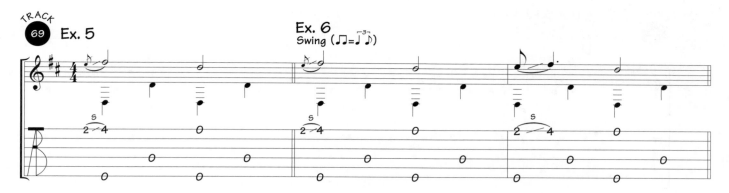

COMBINING FRETTED NOTES WITH SLIDE NOTES

Having a slide on your finger doesn't mean you have to play every note that isn't an open string with the slide. In fact, it sounds really good to mix up fretted notes and slide notes over an alternating bass. You can combine the two over a shuffle as well—think back to the turnaround at the end of the last chapter—but it sounds particularly good with Travis picking.

You *could* play the notes in Example 7 with the slide, but we're going to play them as fretted notes for the time being. One reason to fret these notes is that it's easier to get notes on the second string to sound clean with your fingers instead of the slide. Also, as we'll see in a minute, fretting these notes over the I chord will work particularly well when we play fretted chords for the IV and V chords. (No, we haven't done fretted chords yet. But we will shortly—stay tuned.)

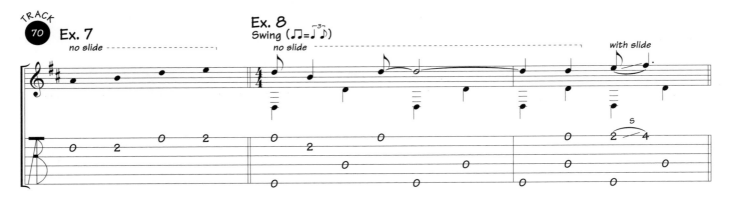

How does it work? Check out Example 8. Fret the melody in measure 1 with your fingers before answering it in measure 2 with the slide lick.

A good way to get used to slipping back and forth between playing fretted and slide notes is to play through a call-and-response idea as in our next song, "Slidin' and Frettin'." The slide phrases (the calls) in measures 1–2 and 5–6 are answered by the fretted licks (the responses) in measures 3–4 and 7–8.

SLIDIN' AND FRETTIN'

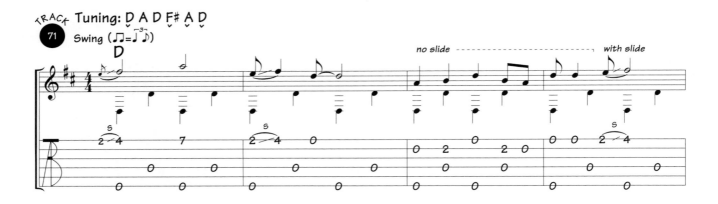

OPEN-POSITION CHORD VOICINGS

So far, whether in D or G tuning, we've always played the IV and V chords with the slide at the fifth and seventh frets, respectively. But open-position fingerings make a lot of sense, for a couple of reasons. For one thing, they make it easier to play and sing at the same time. You can just grab a few notes with your fingers without leaving open position, instead of trying to feel your way up to the fifth or seventh fret while listening for the right pitch, all while you're trying to, y'know, *emote* and stuff with your singing. Also, with the slide straight across the fifth or seventh fret, all we can really get are major chords, but using fretted notes in the open position we can spell out these G7 and A7 voicings:

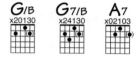

So what is that weird-looking G/B all about? G/B, which musicianly individuals like yourself usually pronounce "G over B," means that you're playing a G chord over a B in the bass. This tells you that you're going to hear not the root, G, as the lowest note in the chord voicing, but something else—in this case, the third of the chord, B.

To play an alternating bass with a G/B fingering, start with your thumb on the fifth string and go up to the fourth, as in Example 9. Once you've got the bass going, you can add in your fingers to play a syncopated pattern over that. If Example 10 seems a little complicated at first, break it down beat by beat to get a handle on it:

Beat 1: Pinch with thumb on the fifth string and finger on the high string, then follow up with a finger on the second string.

Beat 2: Just the fourth string, on the downbeat, followed by a finger on the high string.

Beat 3: Just thumb on the fifth string.

Beat 4: Just thumb on the fourth string.

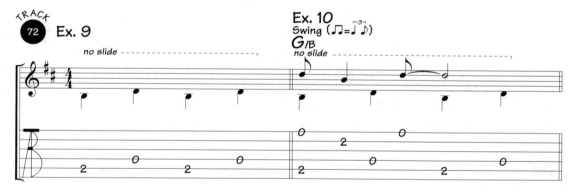

You could play Example 10 as a continuous pattern (while you are singing, for example); that's where the expression *pattern picking* comes from. You could also use the open second string along with the second fret on the second string to get more variation out of this chord shape. Check out the open-to-second-fret move on the second string at the beginning of measure 2 of Example 11: we're really creating a two-measure melodic phrase over the alternating bass instead of just playing through a pattern. If it seems like a lot to wrap your head around, try breaking it down into pinches on the beat and single notes off the beat, just like we did for Example 10.

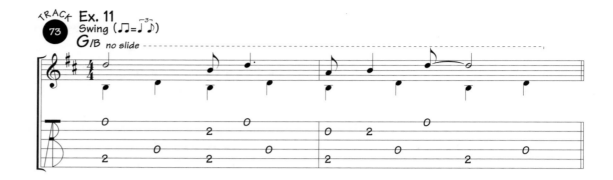

And now, for the big payoff: in Example 12, we're going to use the slide over the I
chord for a measure and then switch to a fretted IV chord in measure 2. Dig, as they
say, how you can stay right in open position after your slide licks and just grab onto
the IV chord:

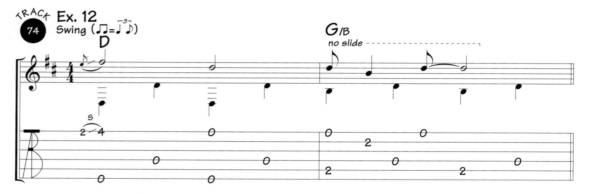

Dave's Helpful Advice is that you grab the G/B fingering (with the second fret on the
fifth string and the first fret on the third string) at the top of measure 2, and then just
drop in your finger on the second fret on the second string when you get there later
in the measure. Why? Well, even though you never pick the middle note of the fingering, it's a critical part of the chord, and it will resonate sympathetically along with the
rest of the notes you *are* picking. If you *don't* fret it, you'll get an additional note that
isn't in the chord—which is usually not a pretty sound.

Now let's look at playing the V chord (A) in open position. First, do just the alternating bass on an open-position A7 chord, as in Example 13. Next, add in your fingers.
Example 14 is a one-measure picking pattern on an A7. Rhythmically, it's the same as
the first picking pattern we did on G/B. Again, Dave's Advice says: fret the whole A7
chord, even if you're not picking every note that you're fingering.

Finally, practice making the switch from a slide lick on the I chord to a fretted voicing on the V chord. You can add in the open high string as a melody note on the way to the second fret of the high string (which is part of the A7 chord).

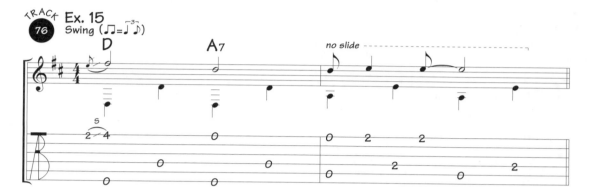

We'll close this chapter with a traditional folk song—two traditional folk songs in one, in fact. Mississippi John Hurt, whose fragrant, rolling fingerpicking style is a whole subject of its own, recorded this tune as "Since I've Laid My Burden Down." Bluegrass and country musicians know the melody as "Will the Circle Be Unbroken." In this arrangement, the melody is played with slide except when it goes down to the second string, where the melody notes are fretted. The only exception to this is measure 14, where the melody is fretted on the high string as part of an A7 chord.

SINCE I'VE LAID MY BURDEN DOWN

PULL-OFFS, HAMMER-ONS, AND BLUE NOTES

And now, as an extra treat for plowing through seven chapters so far, you get to retune your guitar again, back to open G. Since we already know how to combine the open and closed positions in D, let's do the same thing in open G. Are you retuning? Is it annoying? Have you broken any strings yet? (I'll just keep chatting while you stomp around looking for the wire cutters.)

In G, much of the open-position action is on the third string. That's because the open third string in G tuning is G, the root of a G chord. (In open-D tuning, the high string is tuned to the root, or D.)

Example 1 shows all the basic melody notes going right up the third string in open-G tuning. If the fret positions seem familiar, that's because they're the same as for the melody notes up the first string in open-D tuning. Try sliding into these notes by whole steps, as in Example 2.

Giant of the postwar Chicago blues scene, Muddy Waters.

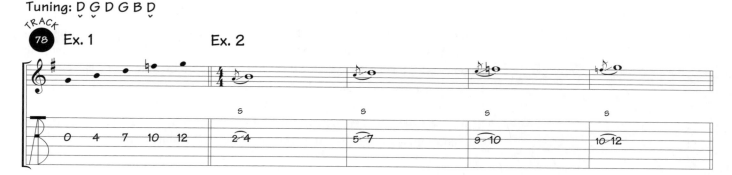

PULL-OFFS

A *pull-off,* as you may know, is that extremely handy technique that allows you to sound two notes but actually pick only one—you pick one fretted note and then pull your fretting finger off the string in a way that sounds a lower fretted note or an open string. With slide, pull-offs aren't that hard to do, and you can use them to sound more fluid when you play in open position. All you really have to do is lift the slide from the strings as you reach your note and the open string will sound, as in Example 3:

Your pull-offs will be only as clean as your technique is in general. That is, if you're still hearing lots of other strings sound as you slide up on a particular string, you're going to hear all those strings ringing open along with the one string you *want* to hear when you lift the slide. So keep paying attention to your damping and muting. Also, make sure you've really reached the fret you were aiming for before you actually lift the slide from the strings. Unless you're going for a quarter-tone slide . . .

QUARTER-TONE SLIDES

This concept is a little more tricky to communicate in print, and even if you listen to the examples in the audio, you may find it difficult at first to hear the difference between a quarter-tone slide and a half-tone slide. Still, it's an important sound, and I wouldn't want you to come away from this book thinking, "Hamburger, that slacker, he never even *tried* to explain quarter-tone slides." So here goes.

To begin with, remember that a one-fret distance on the guitar is called a half-step or a half tone. So a quarter tone is just going to be half of that. "Dave," I hear you say, "how am I supposed to play *half* a fret?" Well, say, what's that on your little finger? A slide? Try this. On the third string, slide from the third fret completely up to the fourth fret (Example 4a). That's a half-step (one-fret) slide, and if you play that over a G bass, the B you're landing on will sound really bright and perfect as the major third of a G chord.

Now slide from the third fret only halfway up to the fourth fret—to an imaginary three-and-a-half fret (Example 4b). Over a G bass, that note won't quite sound major, and it won't quite sound minor. If you just stop right there in the middle, it won't quite sound *right,* either. There's a blue note you're trying to find, and I can really only describe it as being the note on the *way* to the major third. If you haven't lost your patience with this project yet, try this last step: Start at the third fret again and slide toward the fourth fret, but this time *lift* the slide from the strings somewhere between your start at the third fret and your conclusion at the fourth, killing the note mid-flight. You need to be damping behind the slide with your index finger so that lifting the slide actually stops the note; otherwise you'll get a pull-off to the open G.

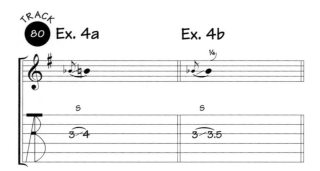

It's a tangy, ambiguous sound, and it does work as a pull-off to the open G string, too. Let's try a few licks with this sound. In Example 5, almost all the action is in the pickup before the downbeat. Example 6 also has a long pickup, this time with a pull-off: make the two quick slides into the seventh fret, and on the second one, lift the slide from the string to get the open G. This open note gives you time to jump down with the slide to the third fret for the last move of the measure.

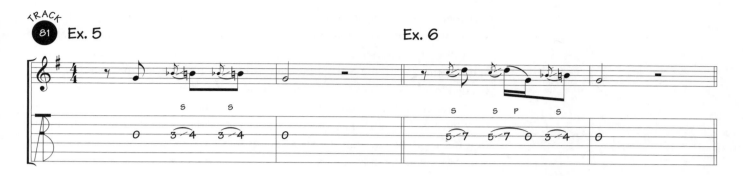

Ex. 5 Ex. 6

Listening to the audio, you might notice that the timing of these two licks feels a little different from what we've been doing in previous chapters, and it's true: all of our melodies until now have been played with what are called *swing eighths* over a shuffle or a two-beat feel, whether the bass notes were being played as quarter notes, alternating bass notes, or shuffled eighth notes. The examples in this chapter are all being played with *straight eighth* notes, which is a very different kind of groove. Example 7 is a classic straight-eighth-note phrase in the style of Muddy Waters. Listen carefully to hear how to phrase the 16th notes at the end of measure 1:

Ex. 7

NOTES ON THE FOURTH STRING

To get more melody notes, we can go down to the fourth string; Example 8 shows the notes that will work (this is similar to the way we went down to the second string to get more melody notes in open-D tuning). Note that the fifth fret on the D string gives us the same pitch as the open third string. As far as playing these notes with the slide, there are a few nuances to consider. Sometimes you want to slide *up to* the F, or from the second fret into the third fret, as in Example 9a. This is generally when you are going from the F *down* to the open D string, as in Example 9b.

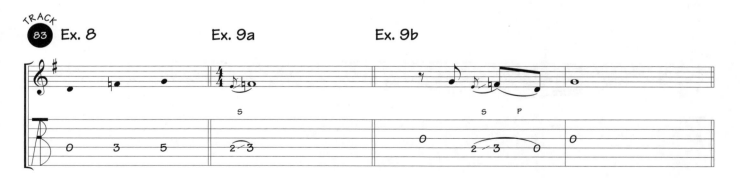

Ex. 8 Ex. 9a Ex. 9b

Other times you want to slide *up from* the F toward a G, as in Example 10a. What you really want is a slide that starts at the third fret and gets cut off on its way to the fourth fret. It's another kind of blue note, like the one we did with the quarter-tone slide on the way to the major third. In this case, you're playing the sound of a note headed for the fourth fret but never quite making it there.

"Dave, man," I hear you say, "that's a little cosmic for a basics book." OK, here's the blow-by-blow mechanics of what to do: Begin sliding from the third to the fourth fret, but lift the slide from the string about halfway there. As you do so, damp the string with your left-hand index finger so you don't inadvertently pull off to the open D string.

Got all that? This works best when your next note is going to be a G, specifically the open G on the third string, as in Example 10b.

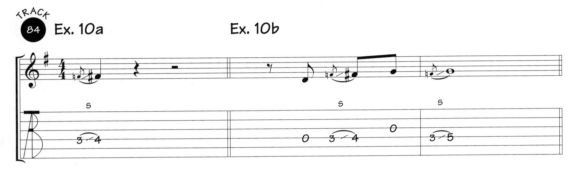

I know, I know, you want to hear how this sounds in real life. And since I am hip to the will of the people, I have prepared "Blue Note Special," a groovy little break in which each phrase is kicked off with a slide up from the third fret on the fourth string:

BLUE NOTE SPECIAL

You can also combine these open-string moves on the third and fourth strings with some of the closed-position sounds we worked on in earlier chapters. Note that back then we were playing closed-position licks with swinging eighth notes; in Example 11, the closed-position licks in measures 1 and 3 are played, like the rest of the solo, with a straight-eighth-note feel:

HAMMER-ONS AND NOTES ON THE FIFTH STRING

Hammering on with the slide, as with regular guitar playing, is the opposite of pulling off. You start by playing an open string, and then drop the slide onto the string to get a second note. Let's go to the fifth string, G, which is an octave down from the third string, and see how this works.

First, just pick the open fifth string, then drop the slide onto the fifth string at the third fret (Example 12a). Now, when I say "drop," I don't mean for you to really *slam* the slide into the strings, because that would create too much additional noise from other strings and result in you actually pressing the strings *to* the fretboard, which is of course not our thing at all. What I do mean is that you need to make contact with the strings in a quick and decisive motion. If you just slowly press into the strings, your index finger (you know, the one you're doing all that excellent left-hand damping with?) will kill the open string's vibration before the slide touches the strings. You *do* want to be using left-hand damping, but if you make your hammer-ons with the slide in a single quick motion, you'll get damping *and* get your hammered-on note ringing out clearly.

And, playing with the slide, we can do things to a note once we've hammered on to it. To play Example 12b, make the same hammer-on move as in Example 12a and then slide up a fret. (Now the hammer-on note itself is just the grace note on the way to the held note at the fourth fret.)

Finally, try following the hammer-on/slide move with an open note on the next string up, as in Example 12c.

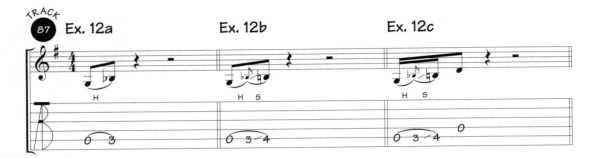

IMPLYING THE IV AND V CHORDS

In certain kinds of early blues, the IV and V chords are merely implied, not actually spelled out with a full chord voicing. The classic move is a single-note pickup riff that lands on the root of the IV or V chord on the downbeat. Example 13 ends on a C, implying a C chord, or the IV; Example 14 lands on a D, implying a D chord, or the V. As you hit the fourth string, shaking the slide with a very heavy vibrato and bearing down on the strings a little harder at the same time will make the upper strings ring out sympathetically, filling out the chord (shown in parentheses).

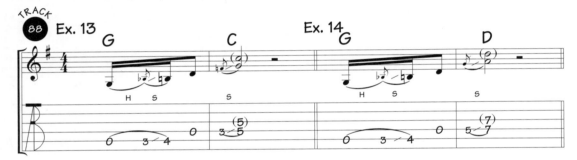

CALL AND RESPONSE BETWEEN CLOSED AND OPEN POSITION

This last example, a 12-bar tune in the style of early Muddy Waters, consists almost entirely of single-note phrases, and yet it's pretty clear what the chord changes are the whole way through. When you're on the I chord, you're generally playing in closed position on the top three strings and answering those phrases with open-position hammer-on licks on the fifth and fourth strings. When you go to the IV chord (measures 5–6) and the turnaround (V chord in measure 9, IV chord in measure 10), everything is happening on the fifth and fourth strings.

There are a couple of particular techniques to watch out for. In the first four measures, every time you land on the third string at the 12th fret, there's a downward slide with no endpoint marked. What you do is this: as soon as you pick the string with the slide at the 12th fret, yank the slide toward the nut, lifting it from the strings somewhere about halfway down the neck. Damp the strings as you lift the slide by letting your fingers leave the strings a little after the slide does. This yank of the slide sounds like Example 15a; when you follow it with the open G string (picked separately) it sounds like Example 15b.

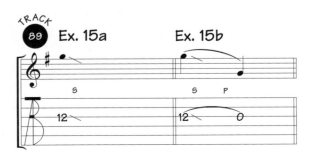

The other thing we haven't really done yet are *double stops*—playing two strings at once. In measure 7 of "Muddy's Blues," you can use one finger on each string, or just brush up on the high string with one finger hard enough to make the second string sound as well.

MUDDY'S BLUES

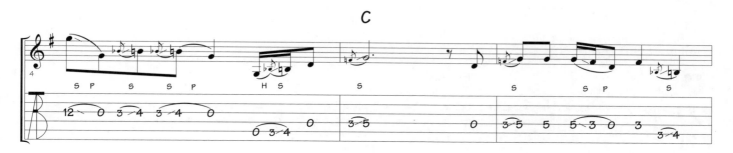

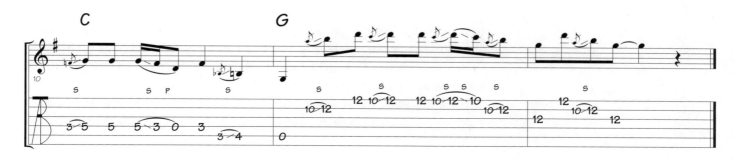

TURNAROUNDS AND MOVING BASS LINES

Guitar player, songwriter, and singer Charley Patton.

As we turn to this last chapter, I hear you say, "Dave, aren't you going to show us any open-position chords in open G? Shouldn't we do more in G with a shuffle feel? What about turnarounds? And can you tell us about descending bass lines?"

Well, funny you should ask, because those are exactly the topics we will cover in this chapter. And since we spent the last chapter working with the straight-eighths feel, let's do everything here with a 12/8 feel, which is heard in many blues styles. You can think of a 12/8 feel as a kind of shuffle, except the pulse comes not from steady swing eighth notes in the bass but from the frequent eighth-note triplets on top. Check out Example 1 to get a handle on the difference between swing eighths, straight eighths, and 12/8. It's easier to read notation in 4/4, but keep the 12/8 feel in mind as you play through the following examples.

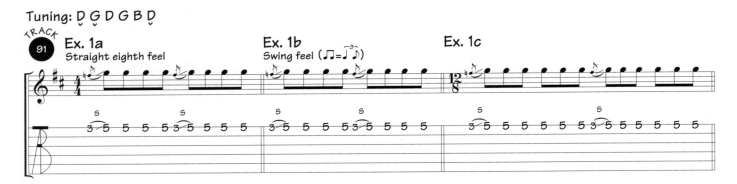

Let's start playing. First, try out these two new voicings. Both of these are to be played without the slide:

Using one picking finger per string—your index for the fourth string, your middle finger for the third string, and your ring finger for the second—play the IV chord (the C) over a steady G bass, as in Example 2. On the second beat, pinch with your thumb and all three fingers, and on the *and* of 2, follow up with just the three fingers.

Using the same right-hand fingering, try coordinating an arpeggiated figure (a series of chord tones played individually) over a steady bass, as in Example 3.

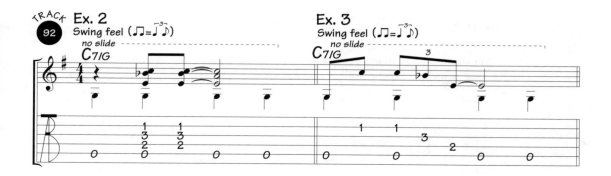

You can break Example 3 down into a series of shorter moves like this:

Beat	Right-hand action
1	thumb (fifth string)
and	ring finger (second string)
2	thumb and ring finger pinch
and	middle finger (third string)
a	index finger (fourth string)
3	thumb
4	thumb

When you get to the triplet on the second beat, count it as "2 and a" instead of just "2 and." I know, it sounds kind of dorky, but it really helps you hear where the beats are falling. Since 12/8 time literally means you're counting 12 eighth notes per measure, you could really count "1 and a 2 and a 3 and a 4 and a" all the way through. In that case, any time you have regular eighth notes, not triplets, they will fall on the 1 and the a. So you could count out Example 3 like this:

Beat	Right-hand action
1	thumb (fifth string)
and	
a	ring finger (second string)
2	thumb and ring finger pinch
and	middle finger (third string)
a	index finger (fourth string)
3	thumb
and	
a	
4	thumb
and	
a	

CHORD ROLLS

You know the way that we're rolling through the strings with our fingers to play an open chord right now? That's called, appropriately enough, a *roll*. Let's try a slightly more elaborate roll over the V chord. You could apply the roll in Example 4 to the IV chord, too:

Play Examples 5 and 6 each as repeated figures to practice forming the IV or V chord on the fly. In both examples you're going from a pickup figure played with the slide into a fretted open chord, and then back into a slide figure.

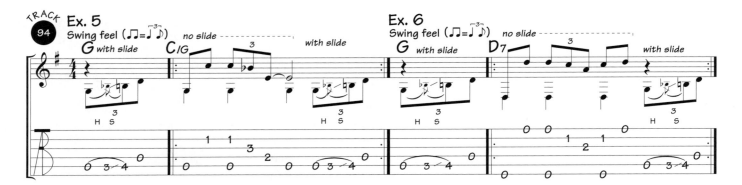

Let's play a blues using these chords. In "Muddy's Blues #2," the triplet figures in measures 1 and 3 establish the 12/8 shuffle feel. The IV chord (measures 5–6) and the turnaround (V to IV, measures 9–10) are played as open-position rolls and include triplets as well. Measure 3 has a kind of elaborate move on the third beat: starting on the third fret of the fourth string, you slide into the fifth fret, then back to the third fret before pulling off to the open fourth string.

MUDDY'S BLUES #2

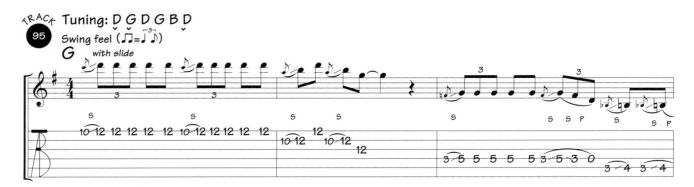

DESCENDING BASS LINES

Descending bass lines are a funky alternative to the steady quarter-note, shuffle, and alternating-bass figures we've done, and now's a good time to learn about them, because some of these licks will work only in open G and not in open D. In open G, we have the low D sixth string *below* the root G on the fifth string. So we can play bass lines that go down from the root to a low fifth. It's pretty slick. Descending lines an octave up on the fourth-string D are also a big part of playing turnaround and various I-chord vamps in G.

The following three examples are all fretted, with no use of the slide. Example 7 is a Son House–style descending bass-line vamp. Grab the fourth and third strings with your index and middle finger, respectively, on every offbeat while your thumb works its way down the sixth string. This can be played straight or swung; we're going to play it straight in this case as well as in Example 10.

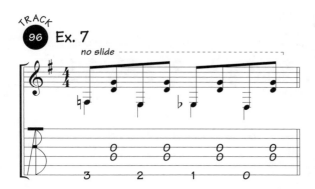

Beat	Right-hand action
1	thumb
and	
a	index
2	thumb
and	
a-a	index, thumb

In Example 8, the descending line is an octave up. Play the notes on the fourth string with your thumb. It's kind of a close pinch, with your index finger just one string over, but picking it this way will help make the next example easier as well. Play this example and the next one with a shuffle feel (swing eighth notes). We're also going to use this figure as a turnaround in the last example of the chapter.

In Example 9 this double-stop figure is broken up into single notes on beat 2. You might think of that combination of one eighth note and two 16ths as a triplet in which the last two notes are rushed in at the end, as shown at left.

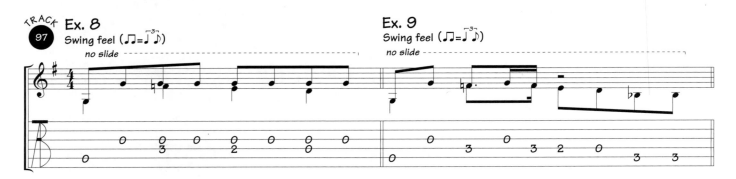

You can build up tremendous momentum using one of these descending bass lines as a repeating figure. In Example 10, using a straight-eighth-note feel, play the figure from Example 7 for measures 1–4. For the slide figures on the IV chord, use a right-hand pinch; your thumb takes the fifth string, your index gets the fourth string, and your middle finger, the third. Continue using your index and middle fingers for the fourth and third strings on the *and* of 2 in measures 5 and 6, and keep the thumb going in steady quarter notes throughout. It looks—and sounds—like you're playing more than just quarter notes with the thumb in measure 6, but you're actually sliding into many of those bass notes without actually picking them. Measures 7 and 8 use a variation on the original bass line.

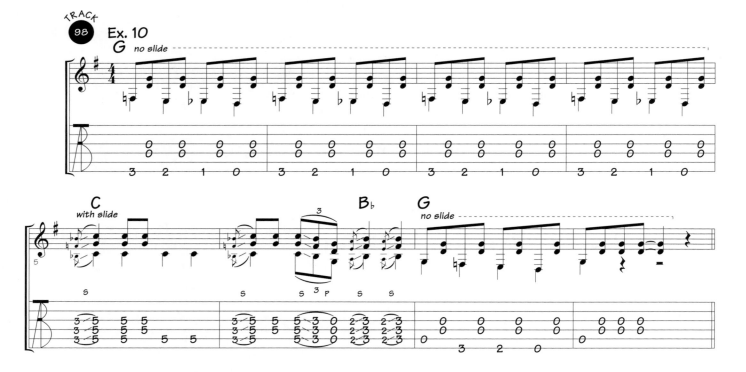

We'll close with one more early Chicago-style 12-bar blues. In "Goin' Back to Clarksdale," played as a shuffle, the figure from Example 10 is the main theme for the I chord. There's an open-position V chord in measure 9 (don't miss the 16th notes) and a sort of IV-to-V-to-♭III riff (C to D to B♭) in measure 10 that's a variation on the IV-chord move in measure 6 of Example 11. And we close things out in measures 11 and 12 with a quintessential G-tuning turnaround.

GOIN' BACK TO CLARKSDALE

FURTHER LISTENING AND LEARNING

RECOMMENDED LISTENING
In cases where more than one recording is listed for an artist, there may be some overlap in material. While the Elmore James and Muddy Waters recordings feature electric slide guitar, both artists were critical figures in the transformation of rural acoustic slide styles into postwar electric blues, and their recordings are an excellent source of bottleneck ideas and vocabulary.

RY COODER
Into the Purple Valley, Reprise 2052.
Boomer's Story, Reprise 26398.
Paradise and Lunch, Reprise 2179.

SON HOUSE
The Original Delta Blues, Columbia 65515.

ELMORE JAMES
King of the Slide Guitar: The Fire/Fury/Enjoy Sessions, Capricorn 42006.

BLIND WILLIE JOHNSON
Dark Was the Night, Columbia 65516.
Praise God I'm Satisfied, Yazoo 1058.

ROBERT JOHNSON
The Complete Recordings, Columbia 46222.

TAMPA RED
The Guitar Wizard, Columbia 53235.
Bottleneck Guitar: 1928–1937, Yazoo 1039.

VARIOUS ARTISTS
The Slide Guitar: Bottles, Knives, and Steel, Columbia 46218.

MUDDY WATERS
The Best of Muddy Waters, MCA 31268.
The Chess Box, MCA 80002.

What's next? Well, if you haven't already, check out some recordings of the great slide guitarists. A short list might include Son House, Robert Johnson, Blind Willie Johnson, Tampa Red, Muddy Waters, and Ry Cooder. As you already know from working with this book's notation and audio tracks, many of the essential nuances of slide guitar really need to be heard to be understood, so listening to records is key. Also, artists like these can help you understand the role of slide guitar as a backup and accompaniment instrument and the relationship between vocals and slide guitar.

Try to figure out some of what you're hearing on records, starting with simple things like fills and little backup figures. Even if you don't get it exactly the same as what you're hearing, your ears will develop from trying. As you try to sort out what's going on, consider whether it sounds closer to D or G tuning, and if it's not matching either one, use a capo to hunt around and see if it's a higher version of one of those tunings. For example, Ry Cooder may play in E or F tuning, which is just D tuning either capoed or tuned up two or three frets; Robert Johnson occasionally played in A or B♭, starting with open-G tuning and raising it by two or three frets.

Note-for-note transcriptions can be a big help with tuning and capoing information, and there are numerous books available; it's obviously most useful to find transcriptions of the actual recordings you're listening to. If you want to be really hardcore about it, you can get some basic tuning information from the transcription, work out as much as possible from the recording itself, and then check what you've figured out against the written transcription. The process takes more time that way, but it's a particularly good way to develop your ears.

Finally, don't forget to just play. Keep a slide near your guitar, and when you're just playing for yourself, making a few noises on the instrument, pick up the slide and see what happens. Don't worry about remembering a particular arrangement or example perfectly; just try to make a little music for yourself, something that sounds good to you.

Learning slide can be a three-dimensional challenge, as you wrestle with fingerstyle coordination, slide technique, and the architecture of open tunings all at once. It's no small feat to have gotten your head, your hands, and your ears all working together on the examples in this book. If you can play the music here, you're already well on your way as a slide guitarist.

ABOUT THE AUTHOR

David Hamburger is a musician and writer who lives in Austin, Texas. He is the author of three other books, including *The Dobro Workbook,* and is a regular instructor at the National Guitar Summer Workshop. A session musician on numerous independent records, Hamburger has also been heard on TFN's *Emeril Live,* on the soundtrack of the PBS film *American Experience: Fatal Flood,* and in the Broadway production of *Footloose.* For a discography, performance schedule, and information on his latest solo CD, *Indigo Rose,* visit davidhamburger.com.

ACKNOWLEDGMENTS

Thanks to the following people for making this book possible: Stedman Hinckley (wherever you are); Peter Keane; Steve James; Paul Rishell; Ben Massey; Carl Thiel; Todd V. Wolfson; Jeff Rodgers, Andrew DuBrock, Stacey Lynn, Trpti Todd, and the rest of the *Acoustic Guitar* staff; Whit Smith; Matt Weiner; and the incomparable Catherine Berry.

This book is dedicated to the memory of my favorite relative, Edward Hamburger (1904–2000).

David Hamburger

NEVER MISS A BEAT

Subscribe to Acoustic Guitar

Get the #1 resource for all things acoustic guitar delivered right to your door.

EVERY ISSUE INCLUDES

- Tips on technique

- Essential gear reviews

- Sheet music for the songs you want to learn

- Interviews with your favorite players

- Lessons to help you become a better acoustic guitar player

- And more

Be the acoustic guitarist you want to be with the magazine for acoustic guitar players, by acoustic guitar players.

Sign up today!